MORE PRAISE
FOR CHUTZPAH GIRLS

LISTED ALPHABETICALLY

"Finally, we can see the array of Jewish accomplishment, commitment, and courage through the prism of the women who are so often unsung! *Chutzpah Girls* is a joy and inspiration to read and look at – and it should be on every young person's bookshelf, regardless of religion."

Abigail Pogrebin, Author of *My Jewish Year: 18 Holidays, One Wondering Jew*

"*Chutzpah Girls* explores the pioneering spirit and ingenuity that drive success. This book is a powerful reminder of the impact that determined, courageous women can have on society, and it serves as an inspiration for readers of all ages to embrace their own inner chutzpah."

Adi Soffer Teeni, CEO, Meta Israel

"The artistry, innovation, and faithfulness to history encapsulated in this volume are simply electric. I can't wait to read it with my children."

Avital Chizhik-Goldschmidt, Writer and Rebbetzin of the Altneu Shul

"Having been raised by strong women and privileged to work with some of the strongest, I applaud *Chutzpah Girls* and will make it my go-to Bat Mitzvah gift for all!"

Ben Pery, CEO, Momentum

"Joy, pride, wonderment, and awe are but a few of the emotions that washed over me as I read these stories of the heroines of our people, culled from 4,000 years of Jewish life until today. I can't wait to read this book with my granddaughters – and grandsons – as each builds their own sense of Jewish pride and sweep of history."

Blu Greenberg, Author and Founder of the Jewish Orthodox Feminist Alliance

"*Chutzpah Girls* is a celebration of the diverse and remarkable Jewish women who inspire us all. The stories highlight bravery, resilience, and the multifaceted nature of our community. A must-read for young readers."

Dr. Mijal Bitton, Sociologist and Spiritual Leader of the Downtown Minyan

"An empowering collection of stories that highlight strong Jewish women and their contributions to the world, and encourages the potential we all can aspire to."

Nikki Schreiber, Founding Editor, Humans of Judaism

"The women in this magnificent book embody the very best of Jewish tradition, inspiring our children to be proud of who they are and teaching them there are no limits on what they can become. A go-to gift for young Jews that should be on every Jewish bookshelf."

Sarah Hurwitz, Author of *Here All Along*, Former White House Speechwriter

"Vivid stories that bring to life remarkable Jewish women whose journeys paint a spectacular portrait of resilience. *Chutzpah Girls* captures the raw energy and indomitable spirit of those who dare to dream and do, igniting the spark of courage in us all."

Sarah Tuttle-Singer, Author of *Jerusalem Drawn and Quartered*

"*Chutzpah Girls* encapsulates the bravery, boldness, and brilliance of Jewish women with stories spanning history, regions, and adversities offering something for everyone."

Sheila Katz, CEO, National Council of Jewish Women

Chutzpah Girls

Toby

Chutzpah Girls

First Edition, 2024

The Toby Press
An imprint of Koren Publishers Jerusalem Ltd.

POB 8531, New Milford, CT 06776-8531, USA
& POB 4044, Jerusalem 9104001, Israel

www.korenpub.com

© Julie Esther Silverstein and Tami Schlossberg Pruwer

Cover and Illustrations: © Koren Publisher Jerusalem, 2024

The publication of this book was made possible
through the generous support of The Jewish Book Trust.

ISBN 978-1-59264-692-0, *hardcover*

Printed and bound in ROT

Julie Esther Silverstein
Tami Schlossberg Pruwer

CHUTZPAH
GIRLS

100 TALES OF DARING JEWISH WOMEN

The Toby Press

DEFINITION

CHUTZPAH

[*hoot-speh*] **noun**

A Jewish superpower: the daring to speak when silenced, to take action when others won't, to try when they say it's impossible, to persevere in times of doubt, to be yourself when it's easier to conform, to stand tall when made to feel small, to believe when it all feels hopeless, to shine your light in the face of darkness.

*"Rabbi Ze'ira said, come and see what **chutzpah** the Land of Israel has, that it produces fruit [in barren land]."*
– Jerusalem Talmud, Taanit 4:5:22

CONTENTS

PREFACE

Welcome to **Chutzpah Girls** – one hundred real-life tales of proud Jewish women who shaped history, rewrote the future, and helped create a better world. When it was hard to be a Jew and hard to be a woman, Chutzpah Girls dared to speak when silenced, pressed forward when stopped, and made their mark when others wanted them erased.

We hope to power up a generation of knowledgeable and confident Jewish kids by zooming in on Jewish women with extraordinary stories across the diverse Jewish experience. We selected Chutzpah Girls from throughout history and around the world who found the courage to survive and thrive against all odds while living deeply Jewish lives. Our stories are not exhaustive biographies. Instead, they explore the responses of Jewish women to challenge. When met with *chutzpah*, the tests we face can be the building blocks of our potential rather than the obstacles that crush our dreams.

Jewish women endured dual discrimination as women and Jews. Our Chutzpah Girls are Sephardi, Mizrahi, Ashkenazi, Persian, Ethiopian, Indian, and Bukharan Jews, persecuted and exiled, who went on to face unequal treatment as women, often succeeding at great personal costs. They experienced aching loss as they gave up dreams to pursue others and persevered through overwhelming doubt when called to lead. Hard work and *chutzpah*, rather than privilege and background, allowed ordinary women to step up in moments of challenge and opportunity to help more women and Jews do the same.

Chutzpah can be defined in various ways. Like any power, it can be a force for good or harm. What a *chutzpah* that one word can mean so many things! It's no wonder it appears throughout the pages of our ancient texts. The Talmud describes the Land of Israel as having *chutzpah*. How else, the Sages wondered, could fruit grow in a barren desert? The women in this book show us that different moments demand distinct forms of *chutzpah* if we are to defeat darkness and spread our light.

Your authors are no strangers to challenge. We dreamed up and wrote this book amidst a global pandemic that kept our children at home, a war that sent our families running into shelters in Tel Aviv and Jerusalem, and the births of two babies, bringing more joy and less sleep into our already busy homes. *Chutzpah* helped us forge ahead – through uncertainty, grief, and exhaustion – to bring these important stories to life.

As there isn't one kind of *chutzpah*, there isn't just one kind of Chutzpah Girl. Some are loud, and others are quiet. Some seek fame, and others prefer anonymity. Some want change, and others embrace tradition. Some win by the sword, and others by the female power of intuition. In this book, we celebrate all Jewish women and believe in the right to equal opportunities so you can create the life of *your* dreams, whether blazing ahead in a profession or lighting the flame of a Jewish home.

Jewish girls today still face challenges. Antisemitism and sexism persist, and the digital world undermines our ability to thrive in the real world, weakening our relationships and self-esteem. We wrote *Chutzpah Girls* so that strong Jewish role models would guide our own sons and daughters as they navigate life's challenges. Even Chutzpah Girls needed Chutzpah Girls! Did you know that Supreme Court Justice Ruth Bader Ginsburg's role models were fellow Chutzpah Girls Emma Lazarus and Henrietta Szold?

But this book is not only about heroes – it's about history. The courage of Jewish women is the through line of the Jewish story. *Chutzpah Girls* will take you on a wild ride through the past and introduce you to key terms, from *achrayut* to Zionism, to help you build your Jewish know-how. When you understand your place in the chain of Jewish history, you can help write the next chapter of our shared future.

More than talking history, we wanted to bring it to life with portraits as bright and bold as the stories they portray. We invited a diverse group of female Jewish artists from around the world to depict the dreams, challenges, and achievements of Jewish women, drawing on their unique talents and perspectives. Who is your favorite? We can't wait to hear.

Now, reach for a blanket, a loved one, and cozy up. This book was meant to be shared – by mothers and daughters – and everyone else. Men and women share an equal role in championing progress. We hope our stories will inspire more Chutzpah Champions so that every Jewish child can walk through the world anchored by eternal Jewish values, a deep knowledge of history, and strong Jewish women *and* men at their sides. May our Chutzpah Girls ignite the *chutzpah* within and help you share your light with the world.

Tami & Julie

SECOND TEMPLE ERA
568 BCE–70 CE

The Royalty: Queens who overcame threats and saved their people from destruction.

Queen Shlomtzion **unifies the Jewish people in peace.**

EARLY MODERN ERA
1492 CE–1790 CE

The Torchlighters: Champions of knowledge, tradition, and spirituality.

Asenath Barazani **leads a yeshivah in Kurdistan.**

TALMUDIC ERA
71 CE–640 CE

The Scholars: Sages who debated Jewish laws and guided Jewish practice.

Yalta **breaks four hundred barrels of wine in a single night.**

ANCIENT ISRAEL ERA
1500 BCE–587 BCE

The Founders: Matriarchs and prophetesses who shaped the Jewish faith.

Sarah **gives birth to the first Israelite at ninety years old.**

MEDIEVAL ERA
641 CE–1491 CE

The Sustainers: Heroes who led the community through golden ages and dark times.

Estellina Conat **is the first woman to print a book.**

CHUTZPAH GIRLS
TIMELINE OF JEWISH HISTORY

21ST CENTURY
2000 CE–PRESENT

The Changemakers: Innovators inspired by the past to create a better future.

Batya Sperling-Milner **uses the first braille Torah trope.**

EMANCIPATION ERA
1791 CE–1899 CE

The Fighters: Warriors for freedom, equal rights, and integration.

Annie Kopchovsky **is the first female global cyclist.**

20TH CENTURY
1900 CE–1999 CE

The Pioneers: Survivors who built the State of Israel and restarted lives in new lands.

Rudolphina Menzel **trains dogs to defend the Yishuv.**

ABIGAIL

ANCIENT ISRAEL ERA | LAND OF ISRAEL
Prophetess

There was danger brewing, and Abigail knew it. As a prophetess, she could predict the future, after all.

Abigail's husband, Nabal, was a difficult and wealthy man who owned thousands of sheep and goats, but there was a rising power in the Land of Israel. David was a respected young warrior and the leader of a growing army.

As Nabal's large flock was easy for robbers to steal, David and his army formed a wall around the flock to keep the sheep and shepherds safe. When David wanted to get paid by Nabal for his help, Nabal not only refused but also insulted David and his army. Furious, David called for his men to take up arms. "Prepare your swords!" He vowed to get back at Nabal.

Hearing word there may soon be a fight, Abigail acted swiftly. She understood that her husband's bad actions could lead the angry army to hurt her family and cause needless bloodshed. She took strategic action to prevent disaster. Without speaking to Nabal, Abigail gathered large amounts of food and set off to find David and his men.

As David's army advanced on Nabal in a burning rage, the brave Abigail met them face-to-face. Instead of drawing a sword, she fell at David's feet. She offered the food as a peace offering and told David that one day, he would become king and wear the crown of Israel. "**God** will make you ruler of Israel. God will destroy your enemies. Don't fight against us with your own hands!"

David stopped his army's march against Nabal and praised Abigail's good judgment to prevent such needless bloodshed. With prophetic words and kind deeds, Abigail calmed hundreds of angry men and saved her family. When she told Nabal everything that had happened, he didn't thank her, as he withheld his thanks to David. Instead, his heart hardened like a stone.

A few days later, God struck Nabal, and he died. Remembering Abigail's wisdom, David proposed to marry her. She accepted and became the wife of the future king of Israel.

"Do not…shed blood needlessly."
– I Samuel 25:31

ADA YONATH

TWENTIETH CENTURY | BORN 1939 | ISRAEL
Crystallographer

Ada was overflowing with questions about the world around her. *How can we see color? Why do we have seasons? What makes the sound of thunder?* Her poor **Jewish** family lived in a single room in a small apartment they shared with two other families in the Geula neighborhood of Jerusalem. But her mind was big, filled with ideas that could not be contained.

At five, Ada's curiosity sparked an experiment to measure the apartment's balcony. With measuring tape in hand, she balanced shakily on a ledge and fell to the pavement below. Ada broke her arm but not her inquiring spirit.

With the encouragement of a teacher who recognized Ada's unique talents, Ada transferred to a special school for bright students. She cleaned, babysat, and tutored other children to help pay for her studies, all while working hard to get good grades.

In university, Ada studied chemistry and later earned her doctorate in X-ray crystallography to discover how to visualize tiny structures like atoms and molecules. She wanted to solve one of the great mysteries of science – how our cells make proteins. Proteins are like factory workers in our bodies. They build muscles, carry oxygen in the blood, and fight off infections. Without them, our bodies can't function properly.

Ada wanted to map the structure of ribosomes, the tiny machines in our cells that make these proteins. Ribosomes were considered impossible to see using X-ray crystallography. "They didn't believe I could do it," she said. But Ada wasn't afraid of hard work.

She experimented under different conditions and, after twenty-five thousand attempts, succeeded in understanding what ribosomes look like and how they do their job. Together with other researchers, she mapped the protein-making process in 3D, helping scientists develop new medicines, like antibiotics, to fight diseases and save lives.

Ada earned a Nobel Prize in Chemistry, the first Israeli woman to receive the prestigious honor. Today, Ada isn't climbing balconies, but she will never stop asking questions.

"I was described as a dreamer. I didn't care."

ADINA BAR-SHALOM

TWENTIETH CENTURY | BORN 1945 | ISRAEL
Education Activist

They pushed the door so hard it nearly flew off its hinges. Adina was only four when the police barged into her Cairo home. Pages of ancient texts flew into the air as the men angrily searched for weapons.

The Israeli War of Independence against Egypt and other Arab countries had started, and the Egyptian government suspected the Jews in Egypt of disloyalty. Adina's father, the well-known and respected community leader Rabbi Ovadia Yosef, had nothing to hide. His home was filled only with books of **Torah**, which seemed to protect him then and always.

As she grew older, Adina too developed a love for books. When she wasn't caring for her ten younger siblings, Adina read all the books she could find. She adored learning and dreamed of becoming a teacher. But like many girls from ultra-Orthodox *haredi* communities, she wasn't allowed to go to high school. She was sent to study sewing instead.

Adina became a successful seamstress and opened a wedding dress shop. But her desire to learn only increased. When her family denied her wish to return to school to study psychology, the science of how people think, feel, and behave, Adina grew determined to expand the possibilities for women like herself.

She spoke out about the state of education in her community, and after years of hard work, she established the first *haredi* college in the world, open to men and women. Adina later entered politics and even created her own political party for the Knesset, Israel's national law-making body. "I wanted to prove that a *haredi* woman could lead," she said.

Thirty years after her wish to study psychology was denied, Adina introduced a degree in psychology at the very college she established. Despite the limits of her upbringing, she managed to knock down closed doors and open up new doors of opportunity for herself and others.

"I'm a go-getter."

ALICE SHALVI

TWENTIETH CENTURY | BORN 1926 | GERMANY
Feminist Educator

Alice was the picture of confidence: an elegantly dressed white-haired woman with a refined British accent; a home filled with friends who swarmed her in admiring conversation; a beloved wife with six children and many grandchildren; and a list of professional achievements that earned her the esteemed title – the mother of Israeli **feminism**. Alice championed the belief that all people, regardless of gender, should be able to pursue their dreams.

Below the surface, however, Alice was filled with self-doubt. As a girl, her family fled Nazi Germany for England on the eve of World War II. In her new school, Alice never felt like the others. "I was an alien. I was a Jew and a foreigner," she recalled.

Alice was an excellent student in her teens and earned admission to a top university, but she never felt she could impress her male professors. She held back in class, fearing that what she had to say was unimportant.

After university, Alice moved to Israel. Throughout her lifetime, no one worked harder to advance the equal treatment of women in every area of Israeli society. She founded the Israel Women's Network to pressure the government to create fairer laws and increase the number of women running for office. She headed a trailblazing school providing a broad education to Orthodox girls. She taught and led the English department at multiple Israeli universities, breaking glass ceilings in higher education.

All the while, Alice never shook the feeling of not being good enough. Many women, even those like Alice, struggle with the fear that they don't belong or can't be successful. While fighting for others on a national stage, Alice's biggest fight was the one deep inside of her. With determination, resilience, and a commitment to her principles, Alice learned to overcome the negative voices and develop the internal strength to forge ahead.

"There's been enormous progress.
There's still a lot more work to be done."

ANGELA BUXTON

TWENTIETH CENTURY | BORN 1934 | UNITED KINGDOM
Tennis Champion

As World War II made its way to England, food shortages left Angela missing the treats she loved, like cakes made of cream and butter. Then came the blackouts at night that kept the city dark to confuse the enemy planes overhead.

But when the bombs started to fall, her family packed their bags and fled to faraway South Africa. There, Angela grew up and discovered the sport of tennis. Unfortunately, she also discovered racism – the mistreatment of someone because of their race or ethnicity. When Angela had a playdate with a Black girl the same age, her White neighbors came over to complain.

Angela returned to England after the war, where she excelled in junior tennis tournaments but faced discrimination of her own. Due to **antisemitism**, or hate against Jewish people, the top tennis training centers rejected her. "You're not going to join the club," they told her. "Why? Am I not good enough?" Angela asked. It was simply because she was a Jew.

For this reason, Angela trained alone and found it challenging to find practice partners. At a tournament in India, Angela noticed that Althea Gibson, an African American tennis player, also spent much of her time alone. She remembered the racism she witnessed as a girl in South Africa and sat down next to Althea. The two women quickly became friends. "We did everything together," Angela recalled.

Jewish women like Angela and women of color like Althea both struggled for acceptance in the mostly White sport of tennis. On the eve of the French Open tournament, when neither woman had a doubles partner, Angela invited Althea to join her. The pair won the title, and later that year, they won again at the Wimbledon Championships in England, the first ever for an African American.

The friendship between Angela and Althea continued off the court and throughout their lives, supporting each other through victories and hardships.

"We came together and beat everybody."

ANNALOUISE PAUL

TWENTIETH CENTURY | BORN 1964 | AUSTRALIA
Dancer-Choreographer

Sometimes, we are guided by signs – magical moments we can't explain that lead us down new paths. Sometimes, our signs are not very magical at all. As a girl, Annalouise dreamt of dancing on stage. When she was old enough to get a job and earn some money of her own, a simple chalkboard sign outside a local dance studio was enough to catch her attention. The sign read, "Flamenco!" She decided to give one class a try.

From the first moment, Annalouise felt an immediate connection with flamenco, the passionate and expressive dance characterized by rhythmic footwork, intricate hand movements, and intense emotions. She left her home in Australia to study flamenco in Spain, the country where it began.

There, she learned about flamenco's history. It came about during the time of the **Spanish Inquisition** when King Ferdinand and Queen Isabella expelled the Jews, Roma, and Moors from Spain because they did not follow their rules and were not believers in the Christian religion. As they hid together in caves to practice their customs in secrecy, their sorrows, songs, and steps wove together into a unique art form and a proud culture of defiance.

As Annalouise discovered flamenco's roots, she discovered her own roots, too. Raised by her Ashkenazi Jewish mother, Annalouise decided to locate family on her father's side. "Who are we? Where do we come from? Who are my grandparents?" asked Annalouise. "We're Spanish Jews expelled in 1492," they told her. Flamenco was not just a beautiful dance but part of Annalouise's core being, her DNA. Maybe the chalkboard sign *was* magical, after all.

Annalouise mastered flamenco and danced all over the world. Today, she leads the renowned Annalouise Paul Dance Theatre and choreographs dances inspired by her unique mixed Ashkenazi-Sephardi heritage and the deeply spiritual Sephardi culture embedded within flamenco.

"We carry stories in our bodies."

ANNE FRANK

TWENTIETH CENTURY | BORN 1929 | GERMANY
Diarist

As a little girl, Anne had a big life. She loved playing ping pong and hopscotch, riding her scooter, and going to the movies. She looked forward to visiting her best friend's house for **Shabbat** dinner on Friday nights and celebrating Jewish holidays with her family.

But as the Nazis rose to power, Anne's world began to shrink. New laws that took away freedoms for Jews forced Anne and her family into hiding. They left their comfortable home and moved into a small secret space behind a bookcase above her father's office. Several righteous non-Jews, including a woman named Miep Gies, brought them food and supplies.

In the cramped, shadowy confines of the annex, Anne began to pen her thoughts in a diary. She found strength in the rustling leaves outside a window. "As long as this exists, I cannot be unhappy," Anne wrote. She could see the beauty of life, even in the worst of times.

Inside the annex, days blended into nights, marked by cautious whispers and the constant threat of discovery. Still, Anne's spirit never dimmed. "I don't think of all the misery." She wrote about the future and her dream of becoming a writer.

Tragically, Anne's story was cut short. Betrayed and captured, she and her family were sent to concentration camps. Anne died, but her father miraculously rediscovered Anne's diary, which Miep safeguarded during their imprisonment. He published the diary on Anne's behalf, thus fulfilling her dream of becoming a writer.

Today, *The Diary of Anne Frank* is one of the most widely read books in the world and is proof of the strength of the human spirit. While life sadly narrowed for Anne, through her diary, her strength has inspired millions worldwide. "I want to go on living even after my death," Anne wrote. She most certainly has.

"I still believe, in spite of everything, that people are truly good at heart."

ANNE NEUBERGER

TWENTIETH CENTURY | BORN 1976 | UNITED STATES
Intelligence & Cybersecurity Official

Ladies and gentlemen, please prepare for takeoff. The passengers flipped up their tray tables and secured their seat belts. Barring a few bumps due to rough air, it should have been a smooth flight from Tel Aviv to Paris. It was anything but smooth.

Just after a stopover in Athens, terrorists took control of the plane and flew it to Entebbe, Uganda. It was a terrifying ordeal, but the **State of Israel** launched a daring rescue mission and saved the lives of nearly everyone on board.

As a child, Anne often heard the story of Operation Entebbe. Her parents, American citizens, were on the flight and among those rescued in the mission. The heroic actions by the government and soldiers of Israel inspired Anne to one day work to help the United States protect and save others.

But Anne didn't have professional role models to guide the way. She grew up speaking Yiddish in the ultra-Orthodox community of Borough Park, Brooklyn, where observant women like her didn't work or worked flexible jobs that allowed them to raise children. When she expressed an interest in public service, people said, "*Frum* women don't do that." *Frum* is a term used to describe a very religious or pious person.

But Anne believed that your faith should never hold you back. She excelled in school and, after working in technology for several years, was assigned to work in the US Department of Defense through the highly respected White House Fellows program. Anne then joined the intelligence community, responsible for protecting America against national security and online threats.

After years of distinguished service, she became the first Deputy National Security Advisor for Cyber and Emerging Threats, at the White House.

Despite her busy job, Anne remained a proud, committed Jewish woman and always managed to leave work early on Fridays to be home in time for *Shabbat*.

"I believe that every person – and every woman – should use the talents God gave them."

ANNE ROSS

TWENTIETH CENTURY | BORN 1919 | UNITED KINGDOM
Codebreaker

Click clack click clack click clack. An electrifying rhythm filled the room as Anne's lightning-fast fingers set the keyboard ablaze. It was the height of World War II, and Anne was at the nerve center of a secret group of British codebreakers. In a mansion at Bletchley Park in London, the best brains in the country worked around the clock, unscrambling complex messages written in secret codes to uncover the enemy's next move.

The Golf Club and Chess Society may have sounded like a place for games. It was anything but innocent. The name disguised covert work guiding high-stakes military decisions. Anne feverishly turned out code signals by the minute for professional codebreakers called cryptographers, as well as intelligence officers, translators, and teleprinters demanding precision at a breakneck pace. The atmosphere of the office was energetic and chaotic. "There were clips and papers sliding all over the place!" she said.

Anne was appointed to lead a team of eighty staff members, including a woman whose husband was tragically killed at sea by Germany's formidable battle cruiser HMS *Bismarck*. Anne proudly remembered how the Bletchley staff plotted the *Bismarck*'s course and directed British naval forces to sink the ship.

Anne was one of few Jews at Bletchley Park. At Christmas time, they served the staff a traditional holiday meal with ham, but Anne kept **kosher**. She followed the Jewish laws of eating, which included a ban on pig products like ham. It wasn't a lavish meal, but she filled up on salad and canned fish instead. Anne believed enemy codes should be broken, but not the codes of Jewish law, which she upheld as sacred.

Despite such challenges, Anne was proud of her contribution to the victory of the Allied forces against the Nazis. Many years later, she took her grandsons for a visit to Bletchley Park to show them where "Granny won the war."

"Our work was kept secret for so long it still seems strange to speak freely of it."

ANNIE COHEN KOPCHOVSKY

EMANCIPATION ERA | BORN 1870 | LATVIA
Global Cyclist

Children wobbled on their tiptoes, hoping to catch a glimpse of the amazing Annie through the roaring crowds in front of the Massachusetts Statehouse. She was about to make history as the first woman to set off on a solo cycling trip around the world.

Annie would face many challenges on her journey around the globe, but few would approach the challenges she'd already overcome. Annie was from a poor family of Latvian **immigrants** and grew up in Boston's tenement housing, an overcrowded apartment building that was dirty, loud, and offered little privacy.

When Annie was a teen, both her parents died, and she took responsibility for raising her younger siblings. Now Annie was married to a peddler and had given birth to three children of her own in just four years. While a daunting challenge for most, a bicycle trip around the world offered Annie what she'd never had before – freedom and opportunity.

As she sped away from the statehouse down Beacon Street, Annie loved the feeling of the wind on her face. At that time, bicycles were surging in popularity. Before cars were out on the road, bicycles allowed women like Annie an opportunity to go where they wanted to go, leaving their heavy skirts and corsets behind. On the trip, Annie could also earn money to help support her family. She showcased advertisements on her bike and clothes and even adopted the name of her sponsor, the Londonderry Water Company.

After a few weeks, "Annie Londonderry" had cycled to Chicago and was nearly ready to quit. Winter was coming, and her forty-two-pound lady's bicycle couldn't handle the hills. But she switched out her bike for a lighter men's model and set off again.

She biked streets from Paris to Nagasaki, and upon returning to America by boat, cycled back across the country. Over fifteen months, she overcame bad weather, serious injury, and countless disbelievers. Still, she finished the thrilling journey with over $10,000 in advertising and prize money in her pocket, as fans and her loving family proudly welcomed her home.

"The most extraordinary journey ever undertaken by a woman."
– The New York World newspaper

ASENATH BARZANI

EARLY MODERN ERA | BORN 1590 | KURDISTAN

Rosh Yeshivah

Generations of the Barzani family lived along the mighty Tigris River in the Kurdistan region of Iraq. The Barzanis were legendary **rabbis**, their knowledge flowing like the river, from father to son, generation after generation, until the year no son was born.

Rabbi Shmuel Barzani was a brilliant scholar who built a *yeshivah* in the city of Mosul. He had a large following of students, but the rabbi had only one child, a daughter named Asenath. Unlike girls of the time, who learned to cook and clean, Asenath learned only Torah. She grew up on the knees of sages, always by her father's side, and earned the title *Tanna'it*, a name reserved for the most outstanding scholars of the community.

When the time came for Asenath to find a husband, it was decided that she would marry her father's best yeshivah student. However, the man would have to agree to a groundbreaking condition – Asenath must be allowed to continue her studies, free from the burden of housework. Out of respect for the *Tanna'it*, he agreed.

Asenath became the head teacher of the Mosul Yeshivah, and when her husband died, she became the first female *rosh yeshivah*, the head of a school for serious Jewish learning. She trained students who later led major Jewish communities and became a respected scholar in her own right. Asenath was an authority on Jewish law and also wrote poetry and prayers. According to legend, she even had supernatural powers. She once saved a burning synagogue and its holy books by unleashing a flock of angels with only a whisper. The undamaged synagogue was renamed in Asenath's honor.

We can still hear Asenath's whispers today as Jewish women rise to new levels of leadership and learning in the Jewish world and beyond.

"I was like a princess of Israel. I grew up on the knees of sages. My father taught me nothing but the holy work of studying the Torah, day and night."

ASHAGER ARARO

TWENTIETH CENTURY | BORN 1991 | ETHIOPIA
Ethiopian Activist

The high-pitched cry could barely be heard over the crunching sound of feet trudging hurriedly along the unpaved gravel road. But there, in a patch of shrubs, somewhere along the four-hundred-mile trek from the Ethiopian village of Gondar to the capital city of Addis Ababa, a baby girl was born.

The mother desperately needed to rest, but she kept going. It was no longer safe in Ethiopia for Jews like her. A civil war was raging, the government was close to collapse, and rebels were attacking the capital. Israeli planes would soon arrive, offering safe passage for Ethiopia's Jews to the Holy Land. The mother named the baby Ashager, meaning "go forward" in Amharic. Nothing would stop her from reaching the land of her dreams.

Ashager was one of the youngest babies to arrive in Israel on Operation Solomon, a secret military airlift of 14,325 Ethiopian Jews in thirty-six hours. Seats were taken out of planes to rescue as many of the **Beta Israel** community as possible. One plane even set a world record for the most passengers on a single aircraft.

It wasn't easy to adjust to life in Israel, but Ashager remembered her parents' hopes and those of the generations that came before. "I can actually live the dream of being here, being Jewish, being safe." Today, Ashager is an ambassador for the Ethiopian Jewish community. She proudly shares her story with audiences around the world, online, and at home in Israel. Ashager is the founder of an Ethiopian Israeli heritage center, celebrating the Beta Israel through food, photography, art, music, and lots of dancing. Why do they dance? "We're a happy people!" Ashager explains. "We have so much to celebrate."

"Imagine your entire life you were praying about this place, generation after generation."

BARBRA STREISAND

TWENTIETH CENTURY | BORN 1942 | UNITED STATES
Performer-Director

"Hey, is that a beak on your face?" The kids at school joked about Barbra's nose. They made her feel ugly. They made her feel different. They made her cry. Barbra wanted to leave her unhappy childhood behind and one day break into the glamorous world of show business. She dreamed of becoming a Broadway star. Sadly, the bullying didn't stop. At casting calls, they rejected Barbra for looking "too Jewish." Having a big nose was a negative Jewish **stereotype**. They told her to have surgery to make her nose smaller.

But Barbra never changed her nose. Once when making a music album cover, Barbra's recording company used photo editing to remove the bump on her nose. They thought Barbra would be pleased, but she wasn't. "I like the bump," she said. "That bump and I have been through a lot together." She told the art director to return her nose to its original shape.

With the bump, Barbra became one of the most successful singers, actresses, and film-makers ever, starring in roles from the Broadway stage to the Hollywood screen. She's one of the few individuals in entertainment to achieve EGOT status, winning all four major entertainment awards – an Emmy for television, a Grammy for music, an Oscar for movies, and a Tony for Broadway.

In one of her most beloved roles, Barbra starred as Fanny Brice in *Funny Girl*, a Broadway musical later made into a hit movie. Like Barbra, Fanny struggled as a Jewish teen with a notable nose to break into show business, but like Barbra, Fanny had talent that the world could not ignore and became a star.

In a famous scene, Barbra, playing Fanny, passes a mirror and turns to admire her reflection. "Hello, gorgeous," she says to herself with a smile. She was gorgeous, indeed.

"I became a movie star, even though I didn't fit the conventional image, me with my asymmetrical face, my notable nose, and my big mouth."

BATYA SPERLING-MILNER

TWENTY-FIRST CENTURY | BORN 2007 | UNITED STATES
Inclusion Activist

Batya was filled with nervous excitement as she made her way up to the *bimah*. The biggest moment of her **bat mitzvah** was finally here. She would soon read from the Torah before the women of her community, as some girls choose to do when celebrating this important milestone.

Reading from the Torah could be intimidating for any *b'nei mitzvah*, but Batya faced a particular challenge. She couldn't see the letters. She had been blind since birth.

Batya had already learned Hebrew braille, the system of raised dots used by people with visual impairments to read and write. The Torah, however, is not just read — it is sung. In a *Tikkun*, the practice book used for learning Torah reading, *trope* markings above and below the letters show how each word should be chanted.

Batya discovered that no braille system for *trope* existed, and she didn't want to simply memorize her Torah reading. She wanted to read and chant Torah like any other Jew would.

To help Batya accomplish this, her mom and dad sought the help of an Israeli software engineer. He created braille characters for the *trope* markings that allowed her to read any line of Torah and chant it too.

Convincing her strictly religious community that she could use the new system would be yet another challenge. For centuries, rabbis upheld the value of *seeing* the Torah while chanting it. Batya and her mother, a *rabbanit*, studied the existing Jewish law and argued for change. With Hebrew and *trope* braille now available, old rules needed adapting. Batya's rabbi agreed.

On the day of her bat mitzvah, Batya broke new ground by chanting the Torah using her braille text. She forever changed Torah reading for the visually impaired and showed how modern technology can make ancient traditions available to all.

"Reading from the Torah is amazing. I don't think anyone should be denied that."

BEATIE DEUTSCH

TWENTIETH CENTURY | BORN 1989 | UNITED STATES
Running Champion

It's good to know what you're great at and Beatie does. "I have a talent for running," she said proudly. "God gave me these strengths." No one could argue with that. Beatie is an Israeli national champion in the marathon and half marathon.

At twenty-six, after having four children in six years, Beatie started running to get back in shape. Despite never running a marathon before, she trained four times a week for four months and impressively finished sixth in the Tel Aviv Marathon, with a time of 3:27. She continued running and completed her next marathon while seven months pregnant.

Beatie was nicknamed "Marathon Mother," and the name stuck. "I love it because it reminds me of my true priority," Beatie said. "I am a mother above all." Plus, she joked, what mother doesn't run a marathon every day of her life? Beatie decided to pursue running professionally, with the hopes of qualifying to represent Israel in the Olympics and other elite races.

As an Orthodox Jew, Beatie sees running as an extension of her faith. "Our role in the world is to take the raw material God has given us and use it to the fullest." She wears modest clothing while running, empowered by the idea that female athletes don't have to expose their bodies to win championships.

"There are a lot of messages out there telling runners to look and dress a certain way," she said. "The focus shouldn't be on how your body looks when you run."

Beatie believes that we are each made up of a body *and* soul, a **neshamah**, with a piece of God inside us. She is proud that she can pursue her dreams while remaining true to *all* of herself.

"Fear holds us back. Belief moves us forward."

BELLA ABZUG

TWENTIETH CENTURY | BORN 1920 | UNITED STATES
Political Trailblazer

Bella roared through life like the new elevated trains clamoring through her native New York City. From the time she was a young girl, no one could stop her from doing what she thought was right.

At the age of thirteen, tragedy struck when her father died. As was the Jewish tradition, she wanted to go to the **synagogue** to honor his memory by saying the *Kaddish*, the special Jewish prayer for mourners.

The rabbi tried to send her home. According to custom at that time, the *Kaddish* was said by sons for their fathers, not by daughters. Bella felt that the custom should change. She returned to the synagogue every day that year to recite the prayer for her father by herself in the women's section.

Bella was later elected president of both her high school and college. She loved speaking out for those in need and decided to become a lawyer. At a time when many Americans were angry about their country's involvement in the Vietnam War, Bella founded Women's Strike for Peace and organized a protest of fifty thousand women across sixty cities. It was the largest women's peace protest of the century.

She later ran for a seat in the House of Representatives of the US Congress. She wore brightly colored wide-brimmed hats and led with an equally memorable campaign slogan: "This woman's place is in the house – the House of Representatives."

Bella won and worked tirelessly to protect the environment and help the disadvantaged. She was a champion of equality and civil rights and even challenged a resolution that labeled Zionism as racism. "Zionism is about freedom," she proudly declared. Battling Bella never took off her colorful hats and never stopped roaring for what she believed was right.

"It's what's under the hat that counts."

BENVENIDA ABRAVANEL

MEDIEVAL ERA | BORN 1473 | ITALY
Philanthropist

It was called the Golden Age. For over a thousand years, a large Jewish community flourished in Spain. The oldest and most prominent of these Spanish Jewish families was the Abravanels. They were business leaders and scholars and held high government positions. Don Isaac Abravanel, the head of the family, even served as treasurer to Spain's powerful rulers, King Ferdinand and Queen Isabella.

One fateful day, the king and queen made a shocking decree. The Jews must betray their faith and convert to Christianity or be banished from Spain forever. Don Isaac tried to convince the rulers to change their minds, but it was useless. Along with thousands of brave Jews, the Abravanels chose their faith and left their beloved home behind.

The Spanish Inquisition was a dark time. Longstanding Jewish communities were uprooted, synagogues destroyed, schools shuttered, and libraries burned. But another member of the Abravanel family, Benvenida, the niece and daughter-in-law of Don Isaac, picked up the torch of leadership. Benvenida fled to Italy, where she worked to rebuild Jewish life in the **Diaspora** and create a haven for those who had lost so much.

Without the safety and security of a homeland, Jews were vulnerable. They were far more likely to become enslaved and forced from their homes again. Benvenida worked with important officials to strengthen the position of the Jews in new lands.

She paid ransoms to secure the freedom of over a thousand captured Jews. She enlisted the help of Spanish princess Eleonora di Toledo to fight a Roman decree pushing the Jews out of the Italian city of Naples.

With Jewish life disrupted, she feared Jewish culture would be lost and encouraged the use of the printing press to publish books to spread Jewish ideas. Benvenida knew Jews could survive without a home, but they couldn't survive without their books.

"A model and a symbol of modesty, piety, wisdom, and power."
– Immanuel Aboab, Jewish scholar

BRACHA KAPACH

TWENTIETH CENTURY | BORN 1922 | YEMEN
Humanitarian

In Yemen, a young Jewish orphan faced near-certain death. The brutal Yemenite army would soon draft the boy as a soldier, and he couldn't refuse. As an orphan, he had no rights, no protection, and nowhere to turn. The only way to avoid being forced into the army was to get married.

So, Yosef was engaged to his eleven-year-old cousin Bracha. The couple wed, had three children, and started planning their journey to British Mandate Palestine. They sold everything they owned that couldn't fit on the back of a donkey and made the long and difficult trip to help build the dream of a state in the Land of Israel.

They eventually settled in Jerusalem, where Yosef became a highly respected rabbi and the leader of the Yemenite community. Bracha saw the poverty and suffering of her fellow immigrants and did all she could to help, all day, every single day.

To provide support to their families, Bracha opened an embroidery business to give jobs to the neighborhood women. She fed and clothed the elderly, ensuring their homes were clean and functioning so they could live their days in dignity. She took the young off the streets and gave them the education and skills to provide for themselves, never abandoning those in need.

Soon, Bracha was helping all of Jerusalem's poor. For over half a century, The *Rabbanit*, as she was respectfully called, mobilized an army of volunteers to distribute thousands of Shabbat and holiday food packages across the city.

She opened a *gemach* to loan gowns to brides from low-income families, organized weddings and bar mitzvahs for families without funds to celebrate, and ran a camp for children roaming the streets during summer break.

For these and many other acts of **chesed**, Hebrew for kindness, Rabbanit Bracha was awarded Israel's top honor for charitable work. How did she do it? Her answer never wavered. "With thanks to God."

"May you merit the chance to do many mitzvot."

BRURIA

TALMUDIC ERA | AROUND 200 | LAND OF ISRAEL
Talmudic Scholar

Bruria never forgot the day her father didn't come home. The Romans had announced a law against the teaching of Torah, but her father, the great scholar Rabbi Hanina ben Teradion, bravely ignored the prohibition and was sentenced to death by the brutal Emperor Hadrian. Bruria was heartbroken by the loss of her father, but she brought honor to his memory and became a great Torah scholar in her own right. She is said to have learned three hundred Jewish laws from three hundred teachers in a single day.

Bruria is the only female Torah scholar whose teachings are cited by the Sages. Her name appears four times in the Babylonian **Talmud**, the most important collection of Jewish laws, and is mentioned in the Tosefta, believed to be an earlier work. Her opinion on legal matters was even adopted in rabbinic tradition.

Bruria spoke up when she saw something wrong and showed faith in the most challenging times. She skillfully balanced criticism and compassion when guiding rabbis and scholars on how to interpret complex Torah passages. She is most celebrated for her arguments on religious law, and her correct decisions, two of which are described in the Tosefta.

The rabbis were concerned about the issue of purity. In one example, the Sages asked, "When does an oven become pure?" The son of Rabbi Hanina ben Teradion said, "When you move it." His daughter Bruria said, "When you take it apart."

Her answer suggested that once you disassemble an oven, it is no longer a whole oven and, therefore, can't be impure. When Rabbi Judah ben Bava heard the argument, he said, "The daughter's answer was better than the son's."

With clear-headed wisdom and immense knowledge, Bruria forged a path for women in Torah scholarship. She was the only woman of the Talmud who offered halakhic guidance which was accepted and quoted by the Sages.

"Bruria has spoken correctly."
– Tosefta Kelim Metzia 1:3

BRURIA BENBASSAT DE ELNECAVÉ

TWENTIETH CENTURY | BORN 1915 | ARGENTINA

Zionist Activist

Ke haber? That's the **Ladino** way of saying, "What's up?" Bruria heard the popular greeting countless times in her Sephardic home in Bulgaria, where she grew up speaking Ladino, the language mixing Spanish and Hebrew, used by the Jews who fled the Spanish Inquisition. For generations, her family lived and thrived in the Spanish Kingdom, but the Inquisition forced them from their home and into the Diaspora. They knew there was only one enduring home for the Jewish people – in their historic homeland.

When Bruria grew up, she married a man who shared her dream of returning to the Land of Israel, and together, they set off to build the foundations of a future Jewish state. They joined Kibbutz Tel Hai, a collective farming community of many other Bulgarian immigrants. Happily, they worked long days in the orange fields, but Bruria developed a health condition for which no treatment was available locally. With a heavy heart, they left for Argentina, where her husband's family lived.

Buenos Aires was in its golden age. The capital of Argentina was alive with music wafting up from every street corner, from the *milongas* pulsating with the rhythmic sounds of tango, to the magnificent Teatro Colon, one of the finest opera houses in the world. But Bruria was far from the life of her dreams in the Land of Israel. She felt like a failure.

After time and some tears, Bruria discovered she could make the dream of a Jewish state bloom from Argentinian soil. She became a leader in WIZO, the Women's International Zionist Organization, and traveled nationwide to speak about the cause. She spearheaded important projects, including a Hebrew-Spanish dictionary, and even became a leader in the Jewish global service organization B'nai B'rith until the age of ninety.

Bruria didn't fulfill her dream of living in Israel. Still, she achieved a different kind of *aliyah* – raising the level of love and support for the Jewish homeland among Jews in the Diaspora. Bruria wasn't in Argentina for the music, but she proved to be a virtuoso conductor, orchestrating support to help build the State of Israel from afar.

"How big our moral commitment to the cause of Israel was."

CHANA LEVIEV

TWENTIETH CENTURY | BORN 1928 | UZBEKISTAN
Faith Keeper

Each Friday morning, Chana's hands moved with practiced ease as she folded the dough for the traditional meat-stuffed *manti* dumplings. The *oshpalao* stew simmered on the stove. Although food in Uzbekistan was scarce at times, Friday night dinner was always a feast, filled with elaborate Bukharan dishes.

Chana and her family were **Bukharan** Jews from the Central Asian city of Samarkand. They had lived in the region for over two thousand years, enduring periods of Muslim, Persian, and Russian rule. Though laborious, Chana's Shabbat preparations were a cherished ritual and demonstrated her fierce commitment to tradition.

Overnight, Chana's life and dream of becoming a doctor were upended when her father-in-law was arrested for publicly practicing Judaism. Under Russian communist rule, they had few religious freedoms. He was sent to a Siberian prison. In search of safety, Chana and her husband moved their family to the capital city of Tashkent. It wasn't easy to maintain a traditional Jewish life. Chana homeschooled her eight children and trekked long distances for kosher food for her family and anyone in need.

The family petitioned the government to emigrate to Israel. After ten difficult years, permission was granted. Chana rejoiced in the freedom to practice Judaism openly, but upon arriving in Israel, was troubled to find many Bukharan women detached from their traditions.

She dedicated the rest of her life, even while battling cancer, to spreading the very values that had kept her family connected, like sticking to faith and speaking kindly toward one another. She traveled to Bukharan communities across Israel and taught groups of women seeking to instill Jewish wisdom in their family lives.

Today Chana's granddaughters, Ruthy and Chagit, spend weekdays in the boardroom and Fridays recreating Bukharan dishes for Shabbat with their own families, knowing that the strength of each generation rests on the strength of the Jewish mother.

"Consider your words before you speak. Addressing people with respect is of the utmost importance."

CHANI LIFSHITZ

TWENTIETH CENTURY | BORN 1977 | NEPAL
Global Emissary

With bright red nails and lipstick, Chani might seem out of place in Kathmandu, Nepal, one of the most rugged places on earth. But Nepal is her home.

Without running water or electricity flowing much of the day, Chani and her husband open their home to thousands of visiting Jewish backpackers each year. As a **shelichah**, or emissary of Chabad, the hasidic movement and international Jewish outreach organization, Chani helps create Jewish life in the remote Himalayan Mountains and even hosts one of the world's largest Passover Seders with over fifteen hundred guests.

But Chani does much more than just feed hungry hikers. She saves lives. While breathtaking views and some of the tallest mountains in the world make Nepal a favorite hiking destination for many young Israelis, extreme weather and slippery cliffs create dangerous conditions.

When a hiker got lost during a blizzard storm, Chani and the man's parents devised a solution to help locate lost hikers. As cell phone reception in the mountains is poor, Chani and her team distribute special satellite phones to outbound hikers.

The phones transmit the locations of the hikers to a computer back in Kathmandu, where Chani and volunteers ensure they are staying on course. "The phones tell us exactly where trekkers are when a tragedy hits," Chani explains.

Chani also cares for the local Nepalese children. Kathmandu is a very poor city where many boys and girls have no choice but to beg for money on the street. "I never get used to seeing such poor children," she says. Chani helps to feed them and does whatever she can to get them off the streets and back into school. She also adopted a Nepalese boy and lovingly cares for him alongside her six other children.

> *"Our job is to give of ourselves.*
> *What you have, share."*

CLAUDIA RODEN

TWENTIETH CENTURY | BORN 1936 | EGYPT
Culinary Anthropologist

As a girl, Claudia loved to watch the boats glide gracefully along the Nile River from the balcony of her home in Cairo. But she never stayed outside for long. The aroma of fresh herbs and spices wafting up from the kitchen lured her away from the peaceful view and into the lively dining room of her Syrian and Turkish Jewish family for lemony green vegetable soup, pies stuffed with mashed eggplant, lamb stewed with apricots, and fluffy rice with raisins and pine nuts.

As a teen, Claudia left Egypt to study art in Europe. She enjoyed her studies and new friends but longed for the dishes of her childhood. She searched for ingredients to recreate them in her London kitchen, far from the waters of the Nile.

Within a few years, a dark chapter unfolded for the **Mizrahi** Jews of the Middle East and North Africa. During the Israeli-Arab War in 1956, Jews were expelled from their home countries, including Claudia's family. Entire cultures, rich with stories, music, jokes, traditions, and time-honored family recipes, were at risk of being lost.

Without a home to return to, Claudia started collecting recipes and stories from those expelled. For generations, there had been no cookbooks. Recipes were passed down from mother to daughter. What began as a project to ensure the survival of her own heritage turned into a lifetime of researching Jewish foods from throughout the region.

Claudia has published over twenty cookbooks on Middle Eastern, Mediterranean, and North African cuisine and received major awards for sharing these dishes with the world. But for Claudia, history was personal, and preserving it was her true reward. For the first time, Mizrahi Jewish dishes were on dinner plates everywhere, and the richness of Mizrahi Jewish culture was on the balcony for all to see.

"Every cuisine tells a story. Jewish food tells the story of an uprooted, migrating people and their vanished worlds."

DAUGHTERS OF ZELOPHEHAD

ANCIENT ISRAEL ERA | LAND OF ISRAEL

Equality Activists

Five sisters walked across the shifting desert expanse, feeling their bare feet sink softly into the hot sand. A sudden gust of dusty wind stung their faces and erased the gentle imprint of their steps. The eyes of the sisters, teary with dust, met in fear. Like a passing gust of desert wind, they knew they, too, could be erased.

The sisters Mahlah, Noa, Hoglah, Milcah, and Tirzah grew up in the generation of Jews wandering the desert wilderness after the Jews' liberation from slavery in Egypt and before their entry into the **Land of Israel**. In the wilderness, tragedy struck. The girls' father, Zelophehad, passed away.

Filled with sadness, the sisters faced a serious problem. At that time, sons alone could inherit a family's land and property. Zelophehad only had daughters. All that their father owned would soon go to their uncles, leaving the sisters with nothing – neither a way to earn a living nor a place to live.

They decided to challenge the law. Boldly, the sisters stood up before their leader Moses, the high priest Eleazar, the tribal heads, and the community. "Why should our father's name disappear just because he had no son? Give us the land that was promised to our father," the sisters petitioned.

Uncertain, Moses sought God's advice. "The daughters of Zelophehad are right," God said. "Give them their father's possessions." As a result, a new law was created, giving women the right to inherit.

When the Jewish people entered the Land of Israel, the sisters received all they had been promised. Their courageous activism in the face of difficulty paved the path for women to be more equal, secure, and independent. Their footprints are still visible today.

"Give us a portion of land."
– Numbers 27:5

DEBORAH & YAEL

ANCIENT ISRAEL ERA | LAND OF ISRAEL

Prophetess & Warrior

The sun's glint on the iron chariots cast a blinding glare as they thundered across the plains. The powerful chariots were the pride of Canaanite King Jabin and his ruthless general Sisera. They were also the terror of the Israelites, who had long suffered under the men's merciless reign. Overcome with despair, the Jews cried out to God for help. God answered their prayers by sending the wise and fearless Deborah.

From the shade of a palm tree, Deborah served as a judge, resolving disputes and restoring justice. She urged the Jews to return to their faith and spread the teachings of Torah. But Deborah didn't stay long in the shade. God called on Deborah to lead ten thousand men in a battle against the Canaanites. She drafted Barak as her general and assembled an army from the tribes of Israel.

The enemy army was strong, and Barak was nervous to go. "If you will go with me, I will go; if not, I will not go," Barak said. But the **Prophetess** Deborah foresaw victory and went into battle alongside Barak. She knew that the mighty General Sisera would fall. And he would fall at the hands of a woman.

The battle was hard, but Deborah showed unwavering faith, and a miraculous flood turned the tide in their favor. The wheels of the once mighty iron Canaanite chariots stopped turning, stuck in the mud of the sludgy battlefield.

As the last Canaanite soldiers fell, General Sisera hid in the tent of a Jewish woman named Yael. Yael gave Sisera warm milk to soothe him and help him fall asleep. Then, she killed the hated man. Deborah and Barak praised God for their victory and Yael's bravery. "Most blessed of women is Yael," they sang.

Deborah's prophecy proved true, and for another forty years, her reign brought peace and renewed faith to the people of Israel.

"God will deliver Sisera into the hands of a woman."
– Judges 4:9

DEBORAH LIPSTADT

TWENTIETH CENTURY | BORN 1947 | UNITED STATES
Holocaust Historian

Everything was going according to plan. After years of school, Deborah finally achieved her ambition of serving as a professor of Jewish history at a great university, inspiring students, conducting research, and writing books.

Deborah never expected her face to be featured on the front page of every major newspaper in the world. However, she was willing to pay the price of unexpected fame to fight for the truth in one of the most significant trials in recent Jewish history.

Deborah was a specialist in the fields of **Holocaust** studies and antisemitism. She believed that senseless hatred toward Jews led to tragedies like the Holocaust, when six million Jews were killed at the hands of the Nazis.

She also believed that the same hatred was still alive, and in order to stop it, she needed to make more people aware of the truth. In her book, *Denying the Holocaust*, she accused the English author David Irving of claiming the Holocaust never happened. He sued her for damaging his reputation.

Lots of people told her not to fight. Just ignore it, they said. "But if I lost, it would become illegal to call the world's leading Holocaust denier a denier," Deborah replied. She enlisted the support of a legal team to prepare mountains of evidence to show that the Holocaust did happen. After a dramatic five-year legal battle, Deborah won.

In recognition of her remarkable work in this fight and throughout her career, Deborah was later appointed by President Biden and confirmed by the Senate at the rank of ambassador to serve as America's special envoy on antisemitism. Her mission remains to create a world where all Jews are safe and protected. When faced with a daunting trial, Deborah chose the path of truth and, in so doing, extended her impact from the classroom to the international stage.

"You can't fight every battle, but there are certain battles you cannot turn away from."

Humiliation for Holocaust sceptic

A victory for truth

HOLOCAUST STORY
The Case for O

.S. Justices Let Stand Su   t Revisionist

vo survivors sh
brutality, resis

cist historian
ces £2m bill
libel defeat

A Long
Lesson
n Hate

graced historian
s £2m costs bill
udge brands him
st and anti-Semitic

e right to lie

e Holocaust:
visionists and

evisionists'
ccurrence

Israelis
welcome
the court
decision

A historic victory in the libel courts for Penguin and Deborah Lipstadt against David Irving

Trade hails Penguin's resolve

DOÑA GRACIA NASI

EARLY MODERN ERA | BORN 1510 | PORTUGAL
Philanthropist

They crowded around the bassinet to see the new baby girl. *Beatrice de Luna! Such a regal name!* Little did the admirers know, the tiny baby concealed a big secret. Her name wasn't Beatrice de Luna at all.

The baby was Jewish, and her real name was Gracia, Spanish for the biblical figure Hannah. She was born to a family of conversos, who had to practice their Jewish faith in secret while outwardly appearing as Christians to escape persecution during the Spanish Inquisition.

As she grew up, Gracia kept the family secret and always remembered who she was. She married a fellow secret crypto-Jew, and together, they built a successful trading company. While running the business and raising her family, Doña Gracia devoted herself to **philanthropy** and helped many Jews flee the horrors of the Inquisition.

Using her extensive business connections and vast wealth, Gracia established a network of escape routes throughout Europe. Her trading ships became vessels of hope, transporting Jews from Spain and Portugal amidst crates of spices and jewels. Her agents used secret signals on each leg of the voyage to let the hidden passengers know when it was time to go forward. She created secret passages through the treacherous Alps and provided jobs for refugees in her warehouses until it was safe to move further south.

Gracia's determination to help others also led her to challenge powerful figures like Pope Paul IV, leader of the Christian world and an avowed hater of Jews. When the Pope imprisoned Jews for their beliefs, Gracia orchestrated a boycott of the Pope's private port of Ancona and redirected her own ships to the port of Pesaro. Her act of defiance caused financial ruin and brought the city of Ancona to its knees.

"The heart of her people."
– Samuel Usque, poet

EDITH EGER

TWENTIETH CENTURY | BORN 1927 | HUNGARY

Psychologist-Ballerina

Edith was walking on her hands as soon as she could walk on her feet. She trained hours a day as a gymnast and dancer and was a rising star on the Hungarian Olympic gymnastics team. That is until her world came tumbling down.

When her coaches discovered that she was Jewish, Edith was cut from the team. Nazi Germany had invaded Hungary, and Edith and her family were forced to move to an area only for Jews called a **ghetto**. Next, they were taken to Auschwitz, a horrible place where Jews were sent to their death during the Holocaust.

On her first night in the concentration camp, a Nazi doctor, Josef Mengele, commanded Edith to dance for him. She had no choice but to dance for the cruel doctor, but in her mind, she was dancing at the Budapest Opera House in a Tchaikovsky ballet.

She was free, and it was Mengele who was a prisoner of his own evil choices. Edith became known as "The Ballerina of Auschwitz," but she used the power of her mind to escape the dark realities of the camp and find the strength to live.

The Nazis transported her from one terrible camp to the next. Sometimes, there was nothing to eat but grass. Sometimes, she didn't think she could go on, but she managed to survive, with deep wounds on her body and in her soul.

Edith got help for herself and became a psychologist to help others suffering from very bad experiences, treating patients and teaching students how to treat others. Edith plans never to retire and enjoys traveling the world to share her story of resilience, ending every talk with her signature ballet high kick.

*"You can be a butterfly.
Shed your chrysalis and fly free."*

ELIZA DAVIS

EMANCIPATION ERA | BORN 1817 | UNITED KINGDOM
Campaigner

Eliza loved reading Charles Dickens. But who didn't? He was the most popular novelist of the time. Dickens was a beloved voice for the people, writing honestly and sympathetically about the problems of the poor.

One day, Eliza's admiration turned to distress when she read Dickens's novel *Oliver Twist*. In the book, an "old shriveled Jew" named Fagin taught Oliver, a poor orphan boy, how to steal. Dickens described the character as dishonest and cruel. He referred to Fagin as "the Jew" 257 times!

Eliza was born in Jamaica but moved to England, where she and her husband bought Dickens's former home. Jews in England were recently granted **emancipation** and allowed to become citizens. However, they still faced great prejudice. Eliza believed that Dickens's Fagin character reinforced harmful stereotypes and negative and false ideas about Jews. And she wasn't prepared to let this go unchallenged. So, Eliza picked up a pen.

In a letter to the famous author, Eliza voiced concerns about his portrayal of Jewish characters. At first, Dickens defensively insisted that the character was authentic and that he meant no harm to Jews. But Eliza didn't back down. She reminded Dickens of his global influence and the responsibility that came with it.

Because of Eliza's efforts, Dickens became more aware of the harm caused by his words to the Jewish community, and he revised *Oliver Twist*, significantly reducing the use of the term "the Jew."

In his next book, he even introduced a Jewish character depicted as kind and generous. Dickens's books are still read today, influencing another generation of readers. Eliza's letters demonstrate the power of respectful dialogue and the ability of one individual to make a difference with only a pen.

"To Charles Dickens, in grateful and admiring recognition of having exercised the noblest quality man can possess: that of atoning for an injury as soon as conscious of having inflicted it."

here are other oppresions,
ch heavier other things far
er, than the letters and
Damascus Lebanon
raged a vile
ice against
d Hebrew
great
Dear Mr Dickens,
boldened by your Courtesy
draw to your attention
matter which I find
if not
in my he
so shall at
crude
of my
people
and of
I do so hope

EMMA LAZARUS

EMANCIPATION ERA | BORN 1849 | UNITED STATES
Writer-Activist

Yearning to breathe free, twenty-three **Sephardic** Jews from Spain and Portugal fled religious persecution for the liberties of the New World. At long last, they could openly practice Judaism without fear. The group established the first synagogue in North America, Congregation Shearith Israel, in the city of New Amsterdam.

Centuries later, New Amsterdam would become New York City, and there Emma was born, a descendant of these brave Jewish pioneers. Emma's wealthy father wanted her to fit into American society. She was given a fine education in languages and literature and developed a love of writing. At eleven years old, she began writing poetry. She composed her first book of poems by the age of seventeen.

Despite her early successes, Emma often felt like an outsider. She was sometimes referred to as a "Jewess," a term for a Jewish woman. While not a bad name, it reminded Emma she was different and never fully part of writer circles, even among those she called her friends.

Emma wrote about major events in America, but also the problems of Jews worldwide. In Russia and nearby areas, violent antisemitic attacks called pogroms forced thousands of Jews to flee their homes in fear. As these refugees poured into America, Emma decided to do more than just write. She started organizations to help Jewish American immigrants learn the skills to support their families in a new country.

When France gifted a statue to the United States on America's one hundredth birthday, Emma was asked to write a poem to raise money for the pedestal. That poem, *The New Colossus,* is still inscribed at the base of the Statue of Liberty, welcoming generations of immigrants fleeing oppression and seeking freedom and opportunity just like Emma's ancestors did centuries before.

"Give me your tired, your poor,
Your huddled masses yearning to breathe free."
– From The New Colossus, by Emma Lazarus

EMMY NOETHER

EMANCIPATION ERA | BORN 1882 | GERMANY
Mathematician

Have you ever played the game of dreidel on **Hanukkah**? Did you notice how nicely the dreidel spins? That's because it's symmetrical. All four sides are the same. Now, try to spin something asymmetrical, like a key. It may spin, but not nearly as well.

Little Emmy liked to wonder about such things. She wasn't particularly good at school. When she was growing up, girls took classes in cooking and sewing. Emmy preferred to dance at parties and impress her friends by solving puzzles in record time.

As Emmy grew up, she decided to keep solving puzzles. She applied to study mathematics at a university and was rejected. *No women allowed,* they told her. She convinced the school to let her sit in on classes. She passed all the tests easily and became the first woman at the college to receive a degree in mathematics.

Emmy completed her doctorate in mathematics, but it still wasn't easy as the only woman in an all-male field. They limited her opportunities to teach and did not make her a professor. She wasn't even paid for her teaching.

But Emmy kept conducting research and won the admiration of mathematicians who invited her to work with them on an exciting development – Albert Einstein's Theory of Relativity, a set of ideas that described how space, time, and gravity work together. Einstein's work was still new. It was a puzzle that had missing pieces.

Emmy developed a powerful idea inspired by the way a dreidel spins. She explained using math how symmetry affects energy and movement. Noether's Theorem, as it is called today, solved a critical problem for Einstein's new theory of gravity and revolutionized the fields of both math and physics.

"My methods are really methods of working and thinking, which is why they have crept in everywhere anonymously."

ESTHER

SECOND TEMPLE ERA | AROUND 380 BCE | PERSIA
Queen

In the heart of the vast Persian Empire lived a shy Jewish orphan named Esther. She was as beautiful as a star but was a supporting actress in her own life story. She did whatever people told her to do.

When King Ahasuerus dethroned his wife, Vashti, he chose Esther, among all the women in his kingdom, as his new queen. It was a dangerous time to be a Jew. The First Temple in Jerusalem was destroyed, the Kingdom of Judah dissolved, and the Jews were exiled to foreign lands. In Hebrew, Esther's name means "hidden." She kept her Jewish heritage concealed, even from her husband, the king, as her guardian Mordechai instructed.

Everything changed for Esther when the king's trusted advisor, Haman, hatched an evil plot to kill all the Jews of the empire in a single day. The plan threatened Esther's people and Esther herself. But she was afraid to approach the king and ask for his protection. He might get angry with her, or worse. She could be put to death!

Esther had a choice. She could continue to hide who she really was or reveal her identity to save her people. Esther asked the Jewish community to fast and pray on her behalf. From this spiritual well, she found the courage to face the king and handle the evil Haman.

Rather than outrightly accusing Haman, Esther invited the king and Haman to a banquet she prepared. In this intimate setting, she unveiled her Jewish identity and Haman's vile plot. King Ahasuerus, enraged that his advisor would kill his loyal and beloved queen, ordered Haman's execution and stopped the order against the Jews.

On **Purim,** Jews celebrate Esther's courage. As they fulfill the obligation to hear Esther's story in the Megillah, they remember the strength hidden within each of us to assume a leading role in the story of our people.

"If it pleases Your Majesty, let my life be granted me as my wish, and my people as my request."
– Esther 7:3

FLORA SASSOON

EMANCIPATION ERA | BORN 1859 | INDIA
Businesswoman

At a young age, Flora learned to walk like a queen and talk like a sage. She was the eldest daughter of parents who each came from prominent Iraqi Jewish families and grew up in India, where nothing was spared to give her the best education.

Esteemed rabbis taught her Jewish texts, and tutors instructed her in six different languages in addition to the native Indian dialect. Flora had the upbringing to succeed in the family business but wouldn't get the chance. It was always the men of the family who ran the company. That is, until Flora changed the way things were always done.

Flora was married at fourteen and had three children. When her husband died, the men met to decide which one would take over his business. As her uncles and brothers quarreled, Flora's voice broke through the noise. *I want to lead*, she said.

Despite her family's resistance, Flora took control of the trading company and led the business to new heights, all while living according to **halakhah**. She was a respected Torah scholar, her opinions sought out by leading rabbis, and the first woman honored to chair the Rabbinic College of London's annual meeting.

At home, her lavish banquets for prominent leaders were conducted to the highest kosher standards. When traveling for business, she brought a kosher butcher with her so she could eat wherever she went and a minyan so she could say her daily prayers.

Flora also used her position to help other women decide their own fate. She fought the Purdah laws in India, which forced women to cover their entire bodies, and encouraged equality in Jewish life by leading by example, famously reading from the Torah on a visit to the great synagogue of Baghdad.

"I rejoice that you have, once in seventy years, also honored a woman."

FRIDA ALEXANDR

TWENTIETH CENTURY | BORN 1906 | BRAZIL
Cowboy Chronicler

Mamãe, conte-me novamente a história dos cowboys judeus! Mommy, tell me the story of the Jewish cowboys again, Frida's children begged in Portuguese. They had heard countless tales of the brave pioneers in the hills of Rio Grande do Sul, but always asked for more. At long last, Frida sat down to write her memoir, the story of her rough-and-tumble childhood in the wilds of Brazil.

Frida was born and raised in Filipson, a Jewish farming and cattle colony in Brazil, started by the Jewish Colonization Association led by Baron Maurice de Hirsch. Pogroms and poverty had made life unbearable for her parents in their Russian **shtetl**. One day, they got word of a wealthy Jewish businessman named Baron de Hirsch, who wanted to help Jews leave Europe and establish ranches in the Americas. He offered to pay for their travel, land, housing, tools, and animals.

Frida's parents accepted the offer and joined Filipson, the first such colony in Brazil. Life was filled with tears of joy and pain. The settlers arrived with little experience and faced endless challenges. There were droughts that parched the soil, swarms of locusts that devoured crops, deadly outbreaks of typhoid fever, and threats to their cattle from wild animals and outlaws. Everyone was expected to work, including children like Frida.

While they labored to bring the land to life, however, Jewish life blossomed. The settlers built a synagogue and school where the children learned Judaism and Hebrew alongside Portuguese and mathematics. The community celebrated holidays, followed kosher rules, and gathered for sacred ceremonies, from births to weddings.

The Filipson colony was unable to sustain itself and was eventually abandoned, but it taught lessons and created a shared sense of purpose that contributed to the growing movement for a future Jewish state in the Land of Israel. Frida grew up to become an advocate for Zionism and a volunteer with WIZO, the Women's International Zionist Organization. Through WIZO, she published her memoirs and became the first woman to tell the story of the Jewish cowboys *and* cowgirls of Brazil.

*"Our modest creek rolled year after year…
washing our wounds, sweat, and tears."*

GAL GADOT

TWENTIETH CENTURY | BORN 1985 | ISRAEL

Actress

One night, when Gal was five years old, her parents threw a party on the roof of their home. Unable to sleep, she snuck upstairs, grabbed a hose, and playfully sprayed everyone with water. Gal laughed, recalling the night years later. "I loved the attention. Maybe I was destined to be an actress!"

But Gal never dreamed of being an actress, let alone a global superstar. She was raised in a small Israeli town and didn't even watch TV. At eighteen, Gal's beauty and poise were noticed, and she was invited to compete in the Miss Israel competition. That would be a nice experience, she thought. "I never thought I would win!" She could hardly believe it when they placed the crown on her head.

Gal enjoyed the spotlight and decided to take up acting and modeling. Upon completing her service as a combat instructor in the Israel Defense Forces (IDF), Gal began auditioning for movies. She received parts in a number of Israeli and American films, but her big break came a few years later. Her agent told her she got an audition with a major movie studio. "Have you ever heard of Wonder Woman?" he asked. Her jaw dropped. Gal was cast in the lead role as the famous superhero.

Gal soon proved to be a wonder woman on and off the screen. With her newfound fame, she took up causes close to her heart. She spoke out passionately against antisemitism and the dangers of terrorism. Despite public backlash, she shared the horrors of October 7th and the plight of the hostages taken by Hamas.

Even though Gal became the first Israeli to receive a star on Hollywood's Walk of Fame, she tries to remain a grateful, small-town girl. Every morning, upon waking, she says a **tefillah** in gratitude. *Tefillah* is the Hebrew word for prayer. "I give thanks to God. Nothing is to be taken for granted."

"Wonder Woman has so many powers, but at the end of the day, she's a woman. Her strength is her heart."

GISÈLE BRAKA

TWENTIETH CENTURY | BORN 1920 | TUNISIA
Resistance Fighter

Elegant shoppers in high heels and silk scarves stared into fashion house windows on the Champs-Elysées in Paris, taking no notice as an ambulance pulled up along the grand boulevard. A Red Cross nurse opened the rear double doors, and the passengers scampered out, vanishing into the crowds. They had no interest in shopping. What they wanted could not be bought – freedom.

The Red Cross nurse was named Gisèle. She was a Jew from Tunisia who hid her true identity during World War II to carry out daring acts of **resistance**. Gisèle moved from Tunisia to Paris as a teenager to study nursing. When the Nazis took control of France, Gisèle became a Red Cross nurse to help prisoners of war in holding camps like Drancy and La Croix de Berny. She wore a uniform and had a special pass, which allowed her to move freely throughout the city. Her job was transporting sick prisoners from camps to nearby hospitals, but that was only what it looked like she was doing to the watchful Nazi guards.

In reality, Gisèle used her ambulance as a getaway car, helping hundreds of prisoners escape right under the noses of the Germans. Although her pass allowed transport for two, she took five or six patients at a time and let them off along the Champs-Elysées and the city's busiest boulevards so they could quickly escape into the crowds.

When her secret operation was discovered, she returned to Tunisia, where her resistance continued. Gisèle worked in a military hospital and helped Jews find shelter and food. "I was very naughty in Tunisia, too," she laughed. After the war, Gisèle moved to the newly established State of Israel. She helped Jewish children orphaned by the war make aliyah to Israel and became a diplomat, opening the first Israeli consulate in the country of French Congo.

> *"I was young, I was foolish,*
> *but I did the right thing."*

GLÜCKEL OF HAMELN

EARLY MODERN ERA | BORN 1646 | GERMANY

Yiddish Diarist

I will try to explain everything that has happened to me since my youth.

So reads the diary of Glückel, the earliest known memoir of a woman in **Yiddish**, a language spoken by many European Jews for nearly a thousand years. As a result of good times when they mixed with their neighbors, and difficult times when they were mistreated and isolated, languages like Hebrew and German came together to form Yiddish.

In Yiddish, Glückel's name means "lucky," but her hard work suggests that her extraordinary life was far more than a stroke of luck. Glückel was married at fourteen in an arranged marriage. She went on to have fourteen children and oversaw their care and education, all while helping to run the family jewel trading company. There, she supervised a factory, conducted trade, and forged business relationships throughout Europe. When her beloved husband was dying, he entrusted her to lead the company. "I have no instructions. My wife knows everything. Let her do as she has done until now."

Even with a hugely busy household and company to run, Glückel found time to author her life story. In seven books over thirty years, she covered difficult topics like war and what it was like to be Jewish in her time. She also wrote about happy occasions like weddings and lessons she hoped to pass down. More than just material possessions, she wanted to share the values of independence, family, and tradition with her descendants.

One of Glückel's great-granddaughters, the feminist pioneer Bertha Pappenheim, translated Glückel's memoirs. Bertha founded the League of Jewish Women, the largest Jewish charity of its time, with fifty thousand members. She believed that Glückel's memoirs should be read by every Jewish woman who wants to learn how to balance it all, even in the face of hardship.

"If God wills that I may live to finish them,
I shall leave you my memoirs in seven little books."

GOLDA MEIR

EMANCIPATION ERA | BORN 1898 | UKRAINE
Prime Minister

Golda watched as her father nailed thick wooden boards over their door to keep the family safe during an impending pogrom. Violent attacks on Jews were common in her hometown of Kyiv, Ukraine. She came to see the need for a place where her people could live free from fear.

Golda's family fled to America, and she became the first in her family to graduate from elementary school. With such an opportunity came a sense of responsibility, not just to herself but to others less fortunate. When a classmate couldn't afford her books for school, Golda took action, calling a community meeting and raising the funds.

Golda's parents wanted her to get married and drop out of school, so she ran away and moved in with her sister. She completed her schooling and also found a new classroom – her sister's living room. There, she stayed up late, participating in lively debates about workers' rights and the Jewish future. She became a passionate advocate for the existence of a Jewish state in the Land of Israel and decided to make **aliyah**.

She first lived on Kibbutz Merhavia, where she worked in the chicken coop and picked almonds, but she was plucked from the fields when her talent for politics was discovered. Over the next thirty years, Golda rose through the ranks of government, from labor minister to foreign minister. She eventually served as the first, and so far, only, female prime minister of Israel.

Over the course of her long career, she raised millions of dollars to support the new state, created a strong labor union and national health care system, and built relationships with countries from Europe to Africa. Golda worked to strengthen Israel as a safe haven for Jews and as a light unto the world.

"I was never affected by the question of the success of an undertaking. If I felt it was the right thing to do, I was for it regardless of the possible outcome."

GRACE AGUILAR

EMANCIPATION ERA | BORN 1816 | UNITED KINGDOM
Writer

For much of history, the education of girls was limited. Grace thought this didn't make sense. An English girl, she was born to a Portuguese family that fled the Inquisition hundreds of years before. She understood that Jews had been forced to wander among the nations for centuries, and that it is the Jewish home where our traditions across time and place are preserved. The home is where children are taught, values expressed, and Jewish culture comes alive. And it was clear to Grace that women, especially mothers, as the primary educators, had to be well educated themselves.

From a young age, Grace suffered health problems. She never had her own children. Nonetheless, she became a champion of Jewish mothers. While she was often too weak to walk, her pen became her sword. At the age of seven, Grace started a journal; at twelve, she wrote her first play; and at fifteen, she wrote her first novel. She battled using every form of writing – from poetry and prayer to history and biography – to cast women in the leading roles.

Grace also fought to give women the knowledge to lead a strong Jewish future. She pushed for full access to Jewish texts and an English translation of the **Tanakh**. An English version of Judaism's most important book would allow women who didn't speak Hebrew the ability to read and study the Torah, as well as the Prophets and Writings, which contain well-known stories of heroic Jewish women like Esther and Ruth.

Grace died at a young age and never became a mother, but she breathed powerful new life into old ways of thinking about women's roles in the family and society.

"Religion is not to be worn like a cloak to be put on and off at will. It should be, like the soul, an integral part of the being, becoming one with it, and blending harmoniously with all its thoughts and actions."

Women of Israel

FRIENDSHIP

Vale of Cedars

Magic
WREATH
of
Midd[...]
FLOWE[...]

Spirit of Judah

HANNAH

Believer

Before the *Beit HaMikdash*, the Holy Temple, stood on Jerusalem's Temple Mount, the Israelites gathered to worship at Shiloh, north of Jerusalem. There, on a hilltop plain, stood the stone tablets of the **Ten Commandments** in a portable holy temple called the *Mishkan*.

It was a majestic site that filled the senses. As one passed through a courtyard fragrant with incense, the beauty of the *Mishkan*'s shimmering golden entrance came into view. A symphony of sound filled the air, from the melodic calls of the priests to the loud clamor of public prayers.

But a woman named Hannah took no notice of these sounds and splendors. Married and unable to have children, she was blind to everything but the deepest yearning of her heart – to become a mother. As if that wasn't enough, Hannah was teased by her husband's other wife, who could have children easily. Hannah went up to the *Mishkan* and prayed tearfully to God, vowing that if blessed with a son, she would dedicate his life to God's service. Hannah spoke in her heart, a personal and silent prayer that only God could hear. Her lips moved, but no sound came out.

Standing at the doorpost of the *Mishkan*, the high priest took notice of Hannah and assumed she was drunk. "Sober up!" he scolded. But Hannah was not drunk. "I have had no wine," she insisted. "I have been pouring out my heart to God."

God heard Hannah's prayer and blessed her with a son, Samuel. From a young age, her son served God and became a great prophet who unified the Israelite tribes into a single kingdom. Hannah also left her mark on Jewish tradition. Her prayer became the model for Jewish prayer. When reciting the important *Amidah* prayer multiple times each day, the Rabbis of the Talmud tell us that we must stand and pray silently from our hearts, just as Hannah did.

"The Lord has granted me what I asked of Him."
– I Samuel 1:27

HANNAH RACHEL VERBERMACHER

EMANCIPATION ERA | BORN 1805 | UKRAINE

Hasidic Leader

In the shtetl of Ludmir, a childless couple received a blessing from a great hasidic rebbe and soon gave birth to a beautiful red-haired girl named Hannah.

When she was engaged to marry, Hannah's mother died suddenly just before the wedding. Upon visiting her mother's grave, Hannah tripped over a stone. As she fell, her spirit ascended, and a new one took its place. "I've been given a new and lofty soul," she told her father. "I will devote myself to study." Hannah declined to marry and committed to strict observance of the mitzvot, God's commandments.

Some called her the Ludmir Maiden. Some called her the Ludmir Rebbe, a title given to spiritual masters. She gained a reputation as a scholar and holy woman with the power to work miracles. Like the male hasidic rebbes of her day, she received audiences and presided over traditional gatherings. She also served as a **firzogerin**, leading women's prayers in the Gornshtibl, a synagogue and house of study that she established.

Hannah maintained her modesty, often conducting her teachings through a screen, but as her influence grew, so did opposition from the traditional hasidic community. They were uncomfortable with a woman in such a prominent role. To discredit her, some said she was possessed by an evil spirit. Others said she was possessed by the soul of a *tzaddik*, a righteous man. They insisted that she must not remain unwed.

Hannah was eventually forced to marry, but one after the other, her two marriages quickly ended in divorce. To escape controversy and societal constraints, Hannah immigrated to Ottoman Palestine, in the historic Land of Israel. She reestablished herself in Jerusalem and attracted a diverse group of followers.

Every Shabbat and Rosh Chodesh, the first day of the new Jewish month, they visited their rebbe to listen to her teach words of Torah. Like her biblical namesake, Hannah, Hannah Rachel Verbermacher was not afraid to embrace the power of prayer and dedicate her life to the service of God.

"I transcended the world of bodies."

HELEN SUZMAN

TWENTIETH CENTURY | BORN 1917 | SOUTH AFRICA
Anti-Apartheid Activist

In South Africa, a harsh system known as apartheid separated people with different skin colors and granted them different rights under the law. Black people suffered greatly under apartheid, but Helen, a white Jewish woman, refused to look away.

Like many Jews fleeing **persecution** in Eastern Europe, Helen's family emigrated to South Africa from Lithuania. As a child, Helen was taught to be polite to everyone, regardless of race. However, due to apartheid, she had little contact with black people apart from the housekeepers and gardeners who worked in her home. Helen later came to understand that they had to follow different rules.

When laws were passed preventing black South Africans from moving freely around the country, Helen decided to do something about it. "It was my knowledge of the Jewish experience of persecution that heightened my awareness of the evils of discrimination," she said.

She won a seat in the South African Parliament, where she served for thirty-six years. Throughout her long career, she never stopped fighting the apartheid system. At times, she was the only member of her political party who opposed apartheid laws and the only woman in the Parliament to do so.

Despite facing intense opposition, Helen didn't back down. She used her position to visit places where few white people would go, like black townships and the notorious Robben Island Prison. There, she regularly visited Nelson Mandela, a black anti-apartheid activist, who was imprisoned for his beliefs. When the apartheid system fell, and Mandela was elected the first black president of the new democratic and equal South Africa, Helen celebrated alongside him.

"In the Jewish tradition, justice is very important. The concept of tikkun olam, or repairing the world, is central. It's our duty to try and leave the world a better place than we found it, and that's what I've tried to do."

HENRIETTA SZOLD

EMANCIPATION ERA | BORN 1860 | UNITED STATES
Zionist Leader

Kamelchen. Henrietta's nickname meant "little camel," and she hated it, but the name stuck. Like a camel, little Henrietta was a responsible and hard-working child, always determined to help. She woke up early to bring fresh produce home from the market, cared for her sick siblings, and helped her father write his letters.

Although Henrietta graduated at the top of her class in school, she still appreciated the difficulties that many of her classmates faced as new American immigrants. With better English, they, too, could succeed in school. Henrietta was determined to help. She founded the first English-language adult night school, a model that continues to this day.

On a visit to pre-state Israel, Henrietta was horrified to see starvation and disease among the children of the early Jewish settlement known as the **Yishuv**. They had so many flies swarming around their eyes that they didn't bother to shoo them away. Henrietta understood that the dream of a modern Jewish state in the Land of Israel was possible only with modern medicine.

Returning to America, Henrietta took action. She founded Hadassah, the women's Zionist organization of America, to build the budding region's first modern medical system. Through bake sales and used clothing drives, they raised money to send two nurses to the *Yishuv.* They soon established health clinics, a nursing school, and youth villages to care for children fleeing Nazi Europe.

When a sculptor later created a bust of Henrietta, she told him, "Make my eyes look to the future." In Israel today, Hadassah continues Henrietta's legacy of determined action with nearly three hundred thousand members supporting two world-class research hospitals bringing advanced medical care to Jews and Arabs alike. They support health education, women's initiatives, schools, and programs for underprivileged youth, and like a camel in the desert, they won't stop until Israel is a healthy place for all its citizens.

"Dare to dream, and when you dream, dream big."

HOUDA NONOO

TWENTIETH CENTURY | BORN 1964 | BAHRAIN
Ambassador

On an island in the Arabian Gulf, where modern skyscrapers tower over stones laid by ancient civilizations, Houda grew up in a small Jewish community in the Islamic Kingdom of Bahrain. Contrary to what one might assume, Houda had friends of different religions and backgrounds. Everyone knew she was Jewish, and she never needed to hide who she was. They respected each other's differences and celebrated holidays together, like Passover, Ramadan, and Christmas.

Houda had a wonderful childhood in Bahrain, and she wanted to see all its citizens thrive. She created and led the Bahrain Human Rights Watch Society to help improve the rights of women, children, and domestic workers and served in the government's top legislative body, the Shura Council, as the country's first Jewish female lawmaker.

In spite of being a woman and a Jew in an Islamic nation, the king appointed Houda as Bahrain's ambassador to the United States, marking more firsts for her and her beloved country. She became Bahrain's first female ambassador to the US, its third-ever female ambassador, and the first Jewish ambassador to be appointed from an Arab country.

While in Washington D.C., Houda built bridges, not just between nations but between people, cultures, and religions. One of her proudest memories was hosting the first interfaith *Iftar*, the evening meal eaten to break the fast during the Muslims' Ramadan period of prayer and reflection, with rabbis, priests, and Islamic prayer leaders called imams. It was the first time a Gulf country had done so, and the tradition continues to this day. In addition to starting new traditions, she also changed old ones, including making all-male events open to women too.

With the signing of the Abraham Accords peace treaty between Israel, the United Arab Emirates, and Bahrain, Houda continues to promote **coexistence** in the region and helped found the Association of Gulf Jewish Communities. She is a testament to the belief that our differences don't have to divide us. They can unite us for a better world.

"A culture of peace and collaboration in the region is no longer a wish but a necessity for a prosperous future for all."

HULDAH

Prophetess

The Kingdom of Judah was in trouble. The Judean kings had turned away from God, and idol worship was widespread. The Holy Temple, called the **Beit HaMikdash**, once the center of worship to God, was filled with statues of idols. Torah scrolls were burnt to ashes, and the Temple altar was draped in a shroud of spider webs.

The hated King Amon, the cause of much of this upheaval, was killed by his own servants. With few good options, the people placed his eight-year-old son Josiah on the throne, but unlike his father and family, Josiah grew into a God-fearing leader who opposed idol worship.

In the eighteenth year of his reign, King Josiah took on the enormous task of restoring the Holy Temple. Amid this work, he discovered an ancient Torah scroll from the time of Moses, hidden by the high priests during the days of idol worship.

King Josiah instructed his scribe to read from the Torah. He opened the scroll to a passage in which God warns the Jewish people of the terrible result of neglecting the Torah – destruction and exile from the land. Grief-stricken, the king ordered his messengers to determine whether the words were true.

Although there were other prophets of the time, like Jeremiah and Zechariah, the messengers went to the prophetess Huldah, hoping her compassionate nature as a woman might soften the decree. But Huldah affirmed the truth of the Torah then and for all time. "These are the words of God, and what is written will come to pass."

Huldah's prophecy spurred a spiritual revival in Judah that renewed the covenant with God and ended idol worship. Since her strong show of faith in the words of the Torah, Jews have turned to it as the eternal source of God's teachings.

"Thus said the Lord God of Israel."
– II Chronicles 34:23

IDA NUDEL

TWENTIETH CENTURY | BORN 1931 | RUSSIA

Refusenik Activist

The wind whistled as it whipped through the cracks of the walls in the remote Russian prison. It was Ida's fourth frightful year in the icy Siberian wilderness, but despite the frigid temperatures, terrible disease, and cruel prison guards, nothing could break Ida's spirit.

Once an economist in Moscow, Ida yearned to live in Israel, where she could live freely as a Jew. But when she asked to leave Russia, the government refused, falsely claiming she knew state secrets because of her job. Ida was one of the thousands of **refuseniks** denied permission to move to Israel.

She lost her job but not her determination. Ida led demonstrations and met with foreign leaders. She was arrested many times and eventually exiled to the dreaded Siberia, an icy, remote expanse in northern Russia.

Ida didn't stop fighting. She cared for her fellow inmates and wrote letters to keep the story of refuseniks alive. Her bold actions attracted the attention of people around the world. Over ten thousand people wrote letters to the government protesting her sentence.

Finally, after years of battling the Soviet authorities governing Russia for the right to move to Israel, Ida was granted an exit visa. Before going home to pack for her move, Ida made her way one last time to Moscow's Central Synagogue to stand together with the refuseniks still waiting to leave. She would never stop fighting for them.

When Ida finally arrived in Israel, she was hailed as a hero and greeted by thousands, including Israeli prime minister Yitzhak Shamir. Clutching her new Israeli ID card and brushing away tears, she said, "Some hours ago, I was almost a slave in Moscow. Now, I am a free person in my own country."

"If you are not willing to fight for what you have, you don't deserve to have it."

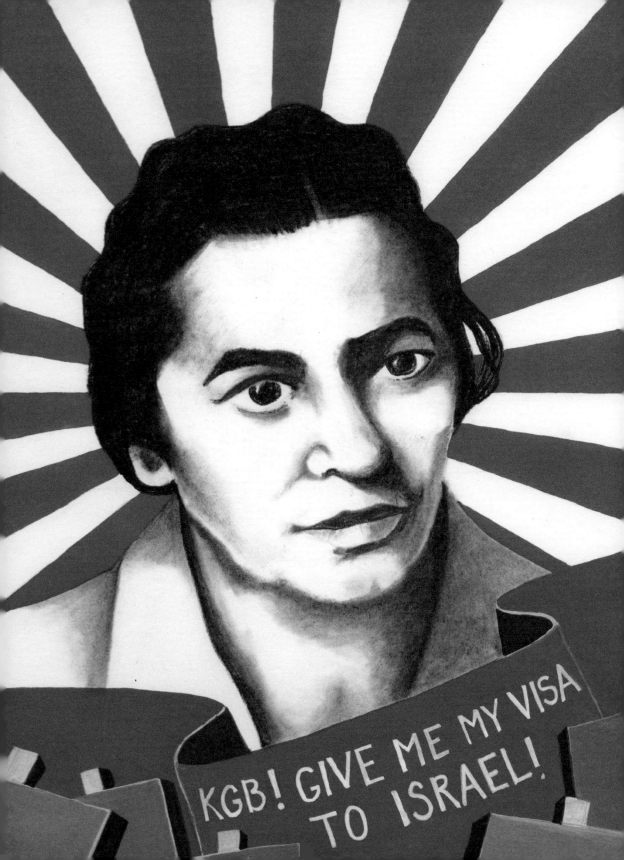

INBAL LIEBERMAN

TWENTIETH CENTURY | BORN 1998 | ISRAEL
Kibbutz Defender

Inbal usually awoke to the sweet sound of chirping birds, but at 6:30 a.m. on October 7, 2023, she was startled from sleep in her bedroom on **Kibbutz** Nir Am by the blare of air raid sirens. Inbal immediately sensed that something was off, and she was right. Hamas terrorists had breached the Gaza border fence in a surprise attack on Israel. The young combat veteran and head of the kibbutz security team sprang into action.

Inbal was the first woman to lead kibbutz security in the Shaar HaNegev area near the Gaza border, and she was well qualified. Inbal was an Israel Defense Forces (IDF) army combat veteran, had grown up on Kibbutz Nir Am, and knew every inch of the land. As the security team leader and the only female on the twelve-member squad, she led the crew with calm control.

On that October morning, Inbal called up her men, handed out weapons, and strategically positioned the team along the kibbutz fence. She then ran from house to house to ensure every family sheltered safely in their fortified rooms. Over a dozen attackers approached the kibbutz, but against great odds, Inbal held them off for nearly three and a half hours until army reinforcements arrived. Not a single terrorist entered Kibbutz Nir Am, and not a single member of the kibbutz was hurt. Nir Am was one of the few communities near the Gaza border that prevented a terrorist invasion on that fateful day.

Some described her as a "one-woman superhero." Inbal's bravery that day was about far more than combat know-how. It was about her responsibility toward the kibbutz community and her country. "She was protecting her home and family," said her father. Inbal was safeguarding the people and the land she loved.

"Inbal is a heroine. Her story leaves no one indifferent – for her coolness, courage, and bravery. Thanks to Inbal, dozens of lives have been saved. Thanks to her, Kibbutz Nir Am was saved."
– Ron Huldai, mayor of Tel Aviv

JUDITH

Warrior

The fearsome Assyrian general Holofernes and his massive army were attacking the **Judean** town of Bethulia. The Jews had valiantly defended their home with all they had, but the city was now under a brutal siege. To force their surrender, Holofernes cut off their food and water supply. The people were on the brink of despair.

Torn between starvation and surrender, the Jews began to lose hope. "If God does not save us in five days, we will give up," they said. But a beautiful young widow named Judith spoke out with unwavering resolve. "If you believe in God, you must never stop trusting. Surrendering is worse than death!" she insisted.

Judith had more than words. She also had a plan to end the siege on Bethulia. She would go to Holofernes herself. Judith took off her mourning garments, adorned herself in fine clothes and jewelry, and walked out through the gates of Bethulia toward the enemy camp. When she arrived, Judith asked to meet with General Holofernes himself. "I am a Hebrew woman," she said. "I will show you how to capture the town."

Holofernes marveled at her beauty and intriguing words. Eventually, she gained his trust, and he invited her to a private feast. Holofernes enjoyed her company and drank more wine than he ever had before. Before long, he passed out on the floor. Judith prayed silently for God's guidance, then unsheathed the general's sword and took aim at his neck. Holofernes was dead.

Judith quickly returned to Bethulia. "Prepare to attack at dawn," she instructed the Jewish residents. And when the sun rose, the Jews attacked. Without General Holofernes at the helm, the Assyrian army fled, freeing Bethulia and all its inhabitants.

"I will do something which will be remembered throughout all generations."
– Judith 8:30

JUDITH LEIBER

TWENTIETH CENTURY | BORN 1921 | HUNGARY

Fashion Designer

A blue butterfly. A slice of watermelon. A green bullfrog. You might think we're at a picnic in the park, but we're actually standing on the red carpet of a movie premiere. The whimsically shaped handbags of Judith Leiber sparkle in the light of flashing cameras as they dangle from the shoulders of famous movie stars. Encrusted in rhinestones and beads, the Leiber is the most wanted handbag in the world.

But it didn't have such a dazzling start. Judith was born to a Jewish family in Hungary. She planned to study chemistry, but antisemitism was on the rise. One of the few places Judith could get a job was at a guild, an association of craftspeople for making handbags. She was hired as an apprentice. First, Judith swept the floors and cooked the glue. Later, she learned to create patterns and mold leather. She became a master craftsperson, and the first woman admitted to the Hungarian Handbag Guild.

But life as a Jew became more difficult. Many of Judith's relatives were sent to **concentration camps,** terrible places where Jews were imprisoned and killed in the Holocaust. To escape, she left her job and hid in a single bedroom along with twenty-six other people. She lived in a ghetto where Jews were separated and forced to endure bad conditions. While war raged and suffering persisted around her, she kept designing handbags – in her imagination.

Judith managed to survive the war and make her way to America with nothing but a toolbox and a mind full of ideas. She worked for handbag makers and then borrowed the money to start her own company.

When a sample purse order arrived tinted an ugly shade of green, Judith covered the color with crystals, giving birth to her now-famous shimmering Leiber bag. She received major awards and international recognition for her creations, many of which can be found on display in museums around the world.

"I have a good sense of humor.
I think everything we do should have whimsy."

JUDITH MONTEFIORE

EARLY MODERN ERA | BORN 1784 | UNITED KINGDOM

Philanthropist

One evening, an elegantly dressed girl was sitting on the cold, hard floor of her family's grand London estate when the front door swung open. In strode Sir Sidney Smith, an admiral of the Royal Navy. He was there to see her father, but his eyes widened in surprise to see such a proper young lady seated on the ground.

For little Judith, it was no ordinary night. It was Tishah B'Av. "This is a day of mourning commemorating Jerusalem's destruction," she explained to the admiral. "It is our custom to sit on the floor and refrain from eating." He bowed his head in respect, inspired by the enduring love of the Jewish people for Jerusalem and the love of one little girl for her Jewish heritage.

Judith grew up between the two worlds of British high society and observant Judaism. Her father was a member of Parliament and an Orthodox Jew. Judith studied Torah alongside literature and languages, a background that prepared her for bridging differences.

Her marriage was no exception. Judith, an **Ashkenazi** Jew with Eastern European roots, was set to marry Moshe Montefiore, a Sephardi businessman with roots in Spain. The synagogue tried to stop them. Ashkenazi-Sephardi marriages were not permitted. But they married anyway, mending deep divisions in the English Jewish community.

Lady Judith also helped to unify global Jewry. She and her husband were equal partners in the most significant philanthropic contributions to the *Yishuv*, the early Jewish settlement before Israel became a state. They used their wealth to rebuild destroyed neighborhoods and construct new ones.

Lady Judith also championed her own projects, from a Jewish orphanage and loan society to restoring the Tomb of Rachel. All the while, she embarked upon a secret personal project to write the very first English-language Jewish cookbook. She wanted to show all British Jews how to enjoy the day's recipes while keeping kosher, too. Boiled gooseberry pudding, anyone?

"Here you can find all the best recipes."
– The Jewish Manual, edited by a Lady

THE JEWISH MANUAL;

OR

PRACTICAL INFORMATION IN JEWISH

AND MODERN COOKERY

WITH A COLLECTION OF

RELATING TO THE TOILETTE

AL OF A VISIT TO PA

Y OF ITALY & THE M

1827-28

JUDY FELD CARR

TWENTIETH CENTURY | BORN 1939 | CANADA
Human Rights Activist

Neighbors could hear the sounds of Beethoven's Symphony no. 5 and the squeals of happy children through the windows of Judy's home in Toronto, Canada. Judy was a musicologist and the busy mother of a young family. Life was perfectly harmonious, yet a storm was brewing in faraway Syria, which she could not ignore.

After the **Six-Day War** between Israel and its Arab neighbors, Mizrahi Jews in those countries faced violence and economic restrictions but weren't allowed to leave. Judy read a news article about the suffering of the Jews in Syria. Although she was far away, she wanted to help. She reached a rabbi in Syria's capital city of Damascus by telegram and began sending boxes of needed supplies, including religious books.

Tragedy struck with the sudden death of Judy's husband. She was now a young single mother with many extra responsibilities, but she redoubled her efforts to help. "What could I do? I had to respond," she said. She stepped away from her musicology teaching and formed a group of volunteers at her local synagogue committed to helping the Jews of Syria who were in danger.

Using religious terms as coded messages, they started a secret communication system with the Syrian Jewish community. Judy's home turned into the hub of an underground escape network to help the Syrian Jews flee to safety. The work was fraught with risks. She negotiated ransoms, planned elaborate escapes, and even smuggled people across heavily guarded borders.

After twenty-eight years of anxious days and sleepless nights, "Mrs. Judy from Canada" saved over three thousand Syrian Jews, and several rare religious books, including the beautiful twelfth century Damascus Keter Tanakh, which she smuggled out in the coat of a Catholic friend and today sits in Israel's National Library.

"It was the best-kept secret in the Jewish world."

KIRA RADINSKY

TWENTIETH CENTURY | BORN 1986 | UKRAINE
Computer Scientist

Cuba hadn't seen a cholera outbreak for over one hundred years. But Kira knew it was coming. She was not a fortune teller or even a medical doctor. She was a computer scientist with a special skill. She could look at large amounts of information to find patterns and make predictions.

Kira had gathered and analyzed years of data on past outbreaks of the bacterial infection. Her research showed that when a poor and dry country has a flood, an outbreak of cholera is likely within a year. Her prediction gave Cuba the time to better prepare for the outbreak and save lives.

As a data scientist, Kira has been able to predict the spread of the coronavirus, the likelihood of a tsunami after an earthquake, and changes to gas prices after a hurricane.

Perhaps not coincidentally, she was born in the Soviet Union, where her life was anything but predictable. "There were food shortages, chemical radiation accidents, and antisemitism," she said. "We always lived with uncertainty." Everything changed for Kira when her family was able to move to Israel. "I had every opportunity."

At age eight, she started computer coding, and by fifteen, she enrolled in the Technion, the prestigious Israeli university for technology, science, and engineering. Kira served as a programmer in a top intelligence unit of the **Israel Defense Forces (IDF)** and returned to the Technion for her doctorate. Later, she worked for top companies and started her own businesses.

From her unpredictable childhood in the Soviet Union to today, Kira is a global leader in the science of using data to make meaningful predictions that help people live healthier and safer lives. Kira has also found welcome predictability in her own life when she gets to spend quality time with her family every week on Shabbat.

"When I was little, they asked me what I would want if I got three wishes. I replied that I did not need three but only one – to know everything."

LALA TAMAR

Artist-Musician

Have you ever peered through a kaleidoscope? Turn it between your fingers and watch a vibrant, ever-changing mosaic, with colorful pieces of glass dancing and multiplying in mesmerizing, intricate patterns.

This dazzling display looks much like Lala Tamar, herself a dynamic cultural mosaic. Born to a Moroccan mother and a Brazilian father in Israel, Tamar's early life was a symphony of languages and music. Portuguese, Arabic, and Hebrew melodies wove together seamlessly, creating a rich tapestry of sound.

In her early twenties, Tamar discovered the language and culture of **Haketia**, spoken and practiced by Sephardic Jews in North Africa. Haketia was a blend of Darija, the Moroccan Arabic her mother spoke, and the Portuguese her father's family spoke. "All of the parts of me came together in Haketia."

She embarked on a mission to resurrect this nearly forgotten language, spending long hours scouring the archives of the National Library of Israel and Hebrew University for recordings of Haketian songs. She lived in Morocco to study traditional Moroccan music and Darija. "I was fascinated by the connection with the Jewish history in Morocco."

Tamar is the first modern artist to record a contemporary album entirely in Haketia. But she not only wishes to preserve it – Lala hopes to reinvent it. Her music is a dance of history and modernity, blending Moroccan glam, Ladino pop, and Haketia world fusion. She celebrates the voices of Sephardic Jewish women across time.

Tamar travels around the globe, promoting the unique sounds of Haketia and Moroccan Darija. But the biggest moment for her was when one of her songs first played on Galgalatz, Israel's most popular radio station. "This was very exciting!" Haketia was out of the archives and back in the streets again.

"Sing your song."

LAURA MARGOLIS JARBLUM

TWENTIETH CENTURY | BORN 1903 | OTTOMAN EMPIRE
Humanitarian

Laura stumbled off the swaying ship in the port of Shanghai. It had been a long journey, and while relieved to arrive, part of her wanted to turn back around and go home. The once beautiful Chinese city was badly damaged by fighting, and the streets were crowded with Jews in desperate need of food, medicine, and housing.

Shanghai may seem an unlikely place for Jews, but when the Nazis invaded Europe, they were forced to run for their lives. Several countries refused to accept Jewish **refugees**, but China did. During the years leading up to and during World War II, about twenty thousand Jewish refugees found safe haven in Shanghai. They often arrived with nothing but the clothes on their backs.

At the height of the war, Laura was sent alone by the Joint Distribution Committee (JDC), an international Jewish aid organization, to organize relief efforts for the Shanghai Jews. Laura had never been to China before, but she drew on a deep well of global experience. She was raised in Constantinople, where her family helped Jews prepare for life in Ottoman Palestine, and had worked in Cuba, where she helped thousands more Jewish refugees.

In Shanghai, Laura got to work. She secured equipment for soup kitchens and set up schools, health centers, and job programs. She bravely negotiated with the military for special permissions, even at great personal risk. When Shanghai was captured by Japan, Laura was even sent to prison. Yet, she managed to smuggle out information on toilet paper to keep the organization's services running.

After the war, Laura left Shanghai and became the first female country leader for the JDC. Over nearly fifty years, Laura's missions took her to conflict zones on three continents and eventually to Israel, where she always helped the most vulnerable.

"What's heroic about doing your job?"

LEAH

ANCIENT ISRAEL ERA | MESOPOTAMIA
Matriarch

In the rolling hills of Mesopotamia, Laban lived with his two daughters, Leah and Rachel. According to the Midrash, stories and commentaries that help explain the Torah, both sisters were beautiful, but Leah had weak eyes damaged by the flood of tears shed for fear she would marry an evil man named Esau.

Leah's life changed when a gentle young man named Jacob arrived at their home. He was Esau's twin brother and in search of a wife. Jacob fell in love with Rachel and agreed to work for seven years to marry her.

Slyly, Laban tricked Jacob. On their wedding night, Laban sent Leah to Jacob's tent instead of Rachel. The following day, Jacob was furious to discover he had married Leah. He agreed to work another seven years to marry Rachel, but the damage to Leah was done. She felt unloved.

Leah tried to win Jacob's affection, but when she saw it was useless, she focused on being grateful for what she had instead of what she lacked. When her son Judah was born, Leah expressed thanks to God for blessing her with children. The Talmud praises Leah's gratefulness. "From the day God created the world, no one thanked God until Leah came and thanked Him."

Leah never felt her husband's adoration, but she appreciated her **berakhot**, the blessings of a loving God. Leah was blessed with seven children – sons Reuben, Simeon, Levi, Judah, Issachar, and Zebulun, and a daughter Dina.

From her son Judah came David, the mighty king of Israel. From her son Levi came the *kohanim*, the revered priests of Israel, as well as the prophets Moses, Aaron, and Miriam. Leah's blessings gave rise to the Jewish nation and a positive outlook that inspires us to see the good in everything.

"God has given me my reward."
– Genesis 30:18

LEAH GOLDBERG

TWENTIETH CENTURY | BORN 1911 | PRUSSIA
Hebrew Poet

Have you ever felt torn between two worlds? Leah did. Her childhood home was in beautiful Lithuania. In winter, the pine trees wore little capes of white snow. In spring, the cuckoo birds sang their special song. But life wasn't easy there for Jews.

Leah's second home was a faraway place she'd never been to, but where her soul longed to be – the Land of Israel. Even as a child, Leah fell in love with the ancient Jewish language of **Hebrew**. She spoke Russian but wrote poems in Hebrew. There was not yet a state for the Jews, but dreamers like Leah were moving to British-controlled Palestine to settle the land. She wanted to be part of the renewal of Hebrew in her ancient homeland.

Upon arriving in Tel Aviv, Leah joined an important group of writers shaping the future of the new Hebrew culture. She published poems, novels, and plays and edited and translated the works of others. She later established and led the Department of Comparative Literature at the Hebrew University of Jerusalem, one of Israel's most prestigious colleges. Today, you can hear Leah's poems in songs by top Israeli musicians. You can read her stories in every Israeli library. You can find her face on Israeli one hundred shekel bills.

Despite success and fame in her new home, Leah, like many immigrants, felt pulled between two worlds. She never forgot the pines of her first home and wrote about them and her feelings of connection to both Lithuania and Israel in her famous poem, *Pine*. In her poem, Leah is the pine tree with roots in two different lands. When you feel torn between two homes or choices, stand tall on deep roots like Leah's mighty pine.

"With you I was transplanted twice,
with you, pine trees, I grew –
roots in two disparate landscapes."
– From Pine, by Leah Goldberg

LINOY ASHRAM

TWENTIETH CENTURY | BORN 1999 | ISRAEL

Gymnastics Champion

The same flags always hung above the Olympic medal podium in rhythmic gymnastics – flags from Eastern European countries like Russia, Bulgaria, and Belarus, which groomed their athletes for gold medals starting at a very young age.

For much of history, girls like Linoy didn't even have a flag to represent them. She was from a mixed Mizrahi, Yemenite, and Sephardic Greek family who had survived centuries of persecution and forced removal from their homes before finding safety in the State of Israel. There, Linoy discovered gymnastics almost by accident.

Linoy's mother was a kindergarten teacher and had plenty of experience with energetic children, but her daughter simply couldn't sit still. She registered Linoy for an after-school sports club to provide an outlet for her boundless energy. Linoy tried a rhythmic gymnastics class and loved it.

Rhythmic gymnasts compete in four events – hoop, ball, clubs, and ribbon. Linoy didn't have fancy equipment at home but had something money couldn't buy – determination. She spent countless hours in the gym, honing her skills, perfecting her routines, and dreaming of one day winning a medal for her country at the Olympics.

At the summer Olympic games in Tokyo, Japan, Linoy proudly performed her ribbon routine to the Jewish folk song **"Hava Nagilah"** and won first place in the individual all-around competition, edging out the Russian favorite. She became the first Israeli woman to win an Olympic gold medal and the first rhythmic gymnast to win gold from a country outside Eastern Europe.

As she stood under the flag of Israel on the Olympic medal podium, Linoy's victory marked a turning point in gymnastics, paving the way for a new generation of young athletes to dream even bigger than they could before.

"Don't let anyone tell you that you can't achieve your dreams."

LORI PALATNIK

TWENTIETH CENTURY | BORN 1960 | CANADA

Jewish Innovator

Her friends weren't so sure about this whole kidney donation thing. "Lori, you have children and responsibilities. Why risk your life?" they pleaded. But Lori was determined. "Why would God give us two kidneys if we can live a perfectly healthy life with one?" she asked them. "Perhaps one to keep and one to give away."

Lori's journey to becoming an organ donor started years earlier when a friend needed a kidney transplant. While her kidney was not a match at the time due to size, it planted in Lori the idea to perhaps donate to someone else. As a result of serious illness, thousands need new kidneys each year, and the waiting list far exceeds the supply. People die every day waiting for a kidney.

One day, Lori was asked if she'd donate her kidney to a stranger. Hesitant at first, she drew on her sense of **achrayut**, the responsibility we have for one another. "For someone I don't know?" she wondered hesitantly. "But someone knows her. This is someone's wife, mother, daughter, friend. Why would I pass up this mitzvah just because I don't know her?" Lori's mind was made up.

She underwent medical tests and was matched with a mother of seven suffering from a life-threatening disease. The transplant was successful, and happily, the recipient went on to live a normal, healthy life.

Today, with just one kidney, Lori does more than most do with two. As founding director of Momentum, a global movement that has sent over twenty-five thousand Jewish women to Israel, she works tirelessly to strengthen the spirit of Jewish women all over the world, for she believes that women, as mothers and leaders, are responsible for ensuring the future of the Jewish people. And she knows from experience and Jewish teaching that if you can save even one life, it is as if you have saved the entire world.

"Even if you don't give a kidney, be a giver – for givers are happy people."

MALKA BRAVERMAN

TWENTIETH CENTURY | BORN 1917 | POLAND
Mossad Official

After Germany's defeat in World War II, Adolf Eichmann, a high-ranking Nazi official, went into hiding in Argentina. During the Holocaust, Eichmann played a major role in sending millions of Jews to concentration camps, where many were killed.

For his crimes, the **Mossad**, Israel's intelligence agency, worked tirelessly to find Eichmann so that he could be brought to justice. Following lead after lead, the Mossad eventually located him. A team of agents captured him near his home and secretly smuggled him to Israel by plane, disguised as an El Al airline crew member. There, Eichmann stood public trial, and the world learned of the atrocities of the Holocaust.

What few knew was that Malka, a top leader of the Mossad, was the brains behind the risky operation. As a teenager living in pre-state Israel, Malka joined the Haganah, the secret Jewish defense organization. At first, she served as a courier passing covert information, but Malka was a quick learner and swiftly rose through the ranks.

After the establishment of the state, Malka was recruited to work for the Mossad, the new national intelligence agency. She directed the agency's spy operations, as well as vital missions like the rescue of North African Jews.

She was tireless in her commitment. Early one morning, Malka gave birth to her daughter, and just a few hours later, she led a meeting in the hospital delivery room with top Mossad officials and army officers at her bedside.

Today, not many people know Malka's name or her contributions to the Jewish people. The Israeli government has revealed few details of her Mossad role. But that wouldn't have bothered Malka. "Anyone who needs to know what I did, knows. That's enough for me," she said. And, for those who knew Malka and her work, she was indispensable.

"The fact is that I reached a very high position."

MARGRET REY

TWENTIETH CENTURY | BORN 1906 | GERMANY
Writer-Illustrator

Margret pressed her ear against the radio to hear the breaking news. The reception was crackly, but the message was clear. **World War II** was coming to France.

Margret and her husband, known by the initials H.A., were desperate to flee the Nazis but had few options. The roads out of Paris were blocked, and the trains weren't running. They managed to find a bicycle shop selling spare parts and cobbled together two working bikes overnight. By daybreak, the couple speedily pedaled out of the city with some essential supplies and their sketches for a children's book about a monkey.

The route to safety was full of obstacles. After France, the couple traveled through Spain, Portugal, and Brazil before arriving in America. Along the way, they were taken in by strangers, hid in a barn, and lost most of their luggage. The monkey in their sketches was also in constant danger. He outran angry firefighters, teetered on telephone wires, and got carried off by helium balloons.

While they saved the story of the monkey, the monkey often seemed to save Margaret and her husband. More than once, they were stopped and searched by police, but the playful drawings charmed the authorities, and the couple was released. Margret and H.A. made it to New York with little money but their drawings intact. One year later, they published *Curious George*. The book was an instant success.

At first, Margret's name was left off the cover to suggest that only a man had written the book, but it was rightly added in later editions. Together, the couple wrote and illustrated each monkey adventure in which Curious George lived out the desires of his creators for freedom and a happy ending.

"Children need dreams and they need heroes. For children, George is both."

MARIA ALTMANN

TWENTIETH CENTURY | BORN 1916 | AUSTRIA
Restitution Activist

For many years, *The Woman in Gold* hung on a wall in the Austrian National Gallery. The dazzling painting by the artist Gustav Klimt showed an elegant woman draped in precious jewelry and an intricate golden gown. She looked like a figure from an ancient mosaic, but the woman in gold was real. Her name was Adele Bloch-Bauer, a Jew from Vienna. And the painting didn't belong to the museum. It was stolen from Adele's family.

When the Nazis took control of Vienna during World War II, they took everything that belonged to the Jews, including works of art. Adele's niece Maria managed to escape but was forced to leave behind the family's beloved painting collection. She settled in America but never forgot her past.

When Maria was an eighty-two-year-old grandmother, she decided it was time to get the paintings back or be repaid their value. She asked for **restitution** from the government of Austria but was refused when they denied her family's ownership of the paintings. They said the paintings didn't belong to her family, but they did.

Maria teamed up with a lawyer to fight for her family's art in court. After seven years, Maria won a remarkable victory. An Austrian judge ruled the paintings be returned to Maria's family. Maria decided to sell the art for $325 million and used a share of the money she earned to support a Holocaust museum and other *tzedakah* projects.

Maria's fight demonstrated to other families who had art stolen from them how they, too, could receive justice. And justice, not money or paintings, was the point for Maria. This fearless grandmother fought a government, stood her ground, and won, proving that it's never too late to right a wrong. Today, you can admire the painting of Adele's aunt, *The Woman in Gold*, at the Neue Galerie in New York City.

"It is not about the money. It is about the principle."

MAYIM BIALIK

TWENTIETH CENTURY | BORN 1975 | UNITED STATES

Neuroscientist-Actress

Mayim may be best known for playing the role of neuroscientist Amy Fowler on the hit American comedy TV show *The Big Bang Theory*. What viewers may not know is that while Amy is a fictional character, Mayim is actually a neuroscientist in real life.

Mayim first rose to fame as a child actress. The movie that launched her career premiered on the very weekend she celebrated her bat mitzvah, and soon after that, she landed the starring role in a long-running TV show, *Blossom*. But when it came time for college, Mayim traded her scripts for textbooks and delved into the study of the brain. She studied neuroscience and earned her doctorate after her first son was born. "I love understanding how we think and feel," she said.

After her role on *The Big Bang Theory*, Mayim combined her stage presence, good humor, and love of learning as a guest host of one of TV's most beloved and longest-running game shows, *Jeopardy!*. But when the bright lights dimmed after a day's shooting on one of her many Hollywood sets, Mayim used her fame to start honest conversations in her books and podcasts about complex topics like mental health.

Mayim grew up in Hollywood and learned that people there are not always as happy and content as they may appear on screen, in celebrity magazines, or on the red carpets of awards shows. Like people everywhere, those in Hollywood can feel sad, even when their lives are going well, or anxious, even when they have little to worry about. Mayim believes we shouldn't be afraid to ask for help when feeling this way. "I've been going to therapy since I was young," she said. "Talking about my feelings and getting help makes me feel less alone."

It's not easy to talk about conditions like depression and anxiety, but Mayim does so because she believes it is her obligation as a Jew. "When we help others feel better, we help to do **tikkun olam** and repair the world," she said.

"Be a light among the nations and share what you have and know with others."

MEERA JACOBS MAHADEVAN

TWENTIETH CENTURY | BORN 1930 | INDIA

Humanitarian

A crying baby lay amidst the rubble of a busy construction site in the Indian city of Delhi. It was no place for an infant. Cranes swung back and forth, and heavy stones fell from the backs of work trucks. But there was nowhere else for the child to go. His mother was a migrant laborer who worked on the site and made so little money that she couldn't afford to pay someone to watch him.

Meera was walking by the construction site when she heard the baby's cry. Meera was part of **Bene Israel**, a community of Jews who lived peacefully in India for two thousand years. She was a novelist and wrote about the strong connection she felt as a Jew to her native country and her Hindu and Muslim neighbors. She believed Bene Israel carried a responsibility to help improve all of Indian society, not just their own community.

Meera ran over to pick up and comfort the baby and quickly realized that other young children were also wandering around the construction site, and this was only one of many buildings going up in the fast-growing country.

Against the sounds of sledgehammers and cement mixers, Meera set up a tent at the site where she cared for the children. She soon created a volunteer organization called Mobile Crèches to create hundreds of childcare centers on construction sites across India. The centers stayed open at night, teaching mothers to read so they could earn better wages and break the cycle of poverty.

Meera's organization is still active and growing fifty years later. It has transformed the lives of one million of India's poorest children and their families.

"The first lesson we learned was that a child cannot be isolated from its family or the community."

MICHELLE FARBER

TWENTIETH CENTURY | BORN 1971 | ISRAEL

Rabbanit

Jerusalem has seen a lot in over three thousand years of history. Still, the city had never witnessed this – a massive crowd of Jewish women gathering to celebrate the completion of a **Daf Yomi** cycle, a seven-and-a-half-year journey of daily Talmud study.

With Talmuds in hand, thousands of women packed the hall, with thousands more joining online, to be part of the *Siyum HaShas* closing ceremony, where Rabbanit Michelle Farber proudly read the blessing for completion on behalf of hundreds of women. As the crowd joined her in a thunderous "*Amen*," she made history as the first woman ever to teach an entire page-a-day cycle of Talmud. That's one page a day for 2,711 days!

For centuries, Talmud study was dominated by men, while women studied other texts or were left out of study altogether. Michelle believed that the Talmud should be a shared treasure, enriching the lives of all who dare to delve into its depths. "The Talmud is the cornerstone of Judaism, and it should be as accessible to women as to men," she said. Even more so, she argued, women have unique perspectives on talmudic debates.

Michelle's mission to bring Talmud study to women began in her dining room. The table where she shares meals with her family became a classroom and recording studio. She created the organization Hadran to revolutionize traditional Talmud study by making it accessible to all online.

The *Siyum HaShas* marked an ending and also a beginning. Michelle is now teaching thousands of new students around the world who hope to join her in completing the next *Daf Yomi* cycle. The end of one cycle heralds the start of the next, reminding us that our study of Talmud is never complete.

"The Talmud is the cornerstone of Judaism, and it should be as accessible to women as to men."

MIRIAM

ANCIENT ISRAEL ERA | EGYPT
Prophetess

A spray of water spattered across Miriam's face as the towering walls of the Red Sea collapsed on the Egyptian army. Once-mighty chariots of bronze, iron, and cedar spun wildly and cracked apart in the powerful currents until the sea calmed and silence fell over the watery battlefield. The Jews had escaped Egypt. After four hundred years of slavery, they were free at last!

Suddenly, a chorus of celebration erupted and broke the stunned silence. Filled with gratitude to God, Miriam picked up a hand drum and led the women of Israel in song. After many years of heartache as slaves, tears of joy replaced tears of pain. The women danced and sang to the rhythm of tambourines to celebrate their newfound freedom.

Miriam's *Song of the Sea* was a song that flowed from within. Her name, Miriam, comes from the Hebrew word for "sea." As a girl, Miriam hid in the watery reeds to keep a watchful eye on her baby brother, Moses, as he floated in a basket down the Nile River. And it was Miriam whose song of praise on the banks of the Red Sea was the first to revive the faith of an oppressed and downtrodden nation.

Later, when the Jews struggled to move forward on their journey through the hot, dry desert without water, it was Miriam's faith that saved them when God produced a well that quenched their thirst. Miriam's well flowed with water for the people until the day she died.

To honor Miriam, some Jews place Miriam's Cup on their **Passover** Seder table and fill it with water to remember that while it was Moses who led the Jewish people to freedom, it was Miriam's faith that sustained them.

"I will sing to God, for He has triumphed gloriously."
– Exodus 15:21

MIRIAM SHAPIRA-LURIA

MEDIEVAL ERA | AROUND 1400 | GERMANY
Talmud Scholar

From behind a drawn curtain, Rabbanit Miriam taught Jewish law to the top students of the Yeshivah of Padua. Today, over five hundred years later, our view still remains obscured of this brilliant scholar of her day, who led the men's yeshivah, gave public lectures on the Talmud, and boldly engaged in debates with important rabbis.

She is mentioned in the writings of her great-grandson, Yochanan Lurie, who recalled her scholarship, her beauty, and how she taught her students from behind a curtain. Perhaps the curtain served to protect her modesty. Perhaps it protected the young men in the yeshivah lest they be distracted from their studies. Or perhaps it was yet another wall for women to get around.

Sadly, we don't know how she felt about the curtain, as none of her personal writings were preserved. This is in stark contrast to her famously learned family. Miriam was a descendant of the great commentator Rashi. She was the sister of the important rabbi, Peretz of Konstanz. She was a grandmother of the Maharshal, a **posek** who decided matters of Jewish law. The Maharshal studied for seven years in his grandmother's yeshivah and learned at her knees.

Libraries of books have been written about these men. You won't find a section on the Rabbanit – only a note or two about her commentaries on difficult passages in the Tanakh and on *piyutim*, or poems that were sung in the synagogue.

Women still have a long way to go to receive full recognition for their achievements. Rabbanit Miriam's story reminds us that the telling of history can change how we remember it. The tellers decide who is remembered and who is erased. We hope that one day, we'll be able to pull back the curtain to learn more about Rabbanit Miriam and the countless Jewish women forgotten in history.

"She sat in the yeshivah behind a curtain and taught the law to some outstanding young men."
– Yochanan Lurie, great-grandson

MORAN SAMUEL

TWENTIETH CENTURY | BORN 1982 | ISRAEL

Paralympic Champion

With fierce determination in her eyes, Moran deftly maneuvered the ball down the court, skillfully dodging opponents and closing the distance to the basket with lightning speed.

Moran was a rising star on the Israeli women's national basketball team, which didn't surprise anyone who'd followed the playing career of the talented young athlete. She played basketball since age nine and earned a spot on the youth national team. During her Israeli military service, Moran was admitted into a special program for top athletes, enabling her to keep playing basketball while serving in the air force.

But, one day, her life and dreams changed in an instant. Moran suffered a rare spinal stroke, blocking blood flow to her spine. This great athlete, who could sprint down the court, was now paralyzed from the waist down. Moran told herself that she was still powerful and strong. She told herself to keep going. After months of rehabilitation, Moran joined the Israeli national women's wheelchair basketball team. It felt great to be back on the court.

Moran's disability also created a new ability – to represent Israel at the Paralympic Games, where athletes with a range of disabilities compete in sports. Moran's partner, Limor, suggested she try rowing. Limor thought Moran would take well to the sport. She was right. Despite the challenges that came with her limited mobility and raising a family of three young children, Moran told herself she could do it. She worked hard and became a three-time Paralympian, two-time Paralympic medalist, and world champion rower. She proudly carried the Israeli flag at the opening ceremony at the Paralympic Games in Tokyo, where she ultimately won a silver medal.

Once, after Moran won a race in Italy, the event organizers didn't have a recording of the Israeli national anthem, "**HaTikvah**," to play as she received her medal. Moran asked for the microphone and sang it proudly from her wheelchair before the cheering crowd.

"Our ability to recover depends on how we speak to ourselves. Positive talk can help you become your own inspiration."

NECHAMA LEIBOWITZ

TWENTIETH CENTURY | BORN 1905 | LATVIA
Torah Teacher

To Nechama, the Torah was a treasure box of questions waiting to be answered. She believed Torah study should be an active adventure and urged her students not to simply understand the meaning of the words but to wrestle with challenges in the text. Torah commentators from Rashi to the Ramban were fixated on resolving these challenges, or *kushiyot. Why does the text use this word? Why is it spelled this way and not that way?* By asking these probing questions and many more, they endeavored to shed light on the deeper meaning of the text.

As a Torah scholar, Nechama wanted her students to wrestle with the *kushiyot* too. "What's bothering Rashi?" Nechama asked. She wanted her students to feel bothered too. Nechama wasn't concerned if her students misunderstood the text. Rather, she was concerned when they thought they understood, but really didn't. "The biggest misunderstanding is thinking there's nothing to understand," she said.

Nechama's approach to Torah was like following a treasure map. After identifying a hard question or *kushiyah*, she guided her students through solutions offered by the commentators and asked them to weigh their strengths and weaknesses. She then encouraged her students to find personal life lessons in the text. She believed that the Torah shouldn't only live in a classroom. It should stay with you and bring personal meaning.

Nechama made Torah study more exciting and accessible to a broader audience. When a group of students wanted to continue learning after the school year ended, she mailed them study sheets with questions on the Torah portion.

Word spread, and over the next thirty years, Nechama's study group reached tens of thousands each week, from secular people who never went to synagogue, to religious men who had never learned Torah from a woman. Nechama earned many honors for her work, but the one most important to her was simply to be called **Morah**, the Hebrew word for teacher.

"Torah study is not about finding answers; it's about asking questions."

NOA TISHBY

TWENTIETH CENTURY | BORN 1975 | ISRAEL
Author and Zionist Activist

Noa has always had a lot to say. A born storyteller, she landed her first television commercial at the age of eight and later starred in and created leading shows in Israel and the United States.

Stories were in her DNA. Noa's family weren't performers, but they played a starring role in the story of the State of Israel. A **Zionist** pioneer, her grandmother was a founder of Degania, the first kibbutz in Israel, and her grandfather was Israel's first ambassador to West Africa.

Noa moved to Los Angeles to advance her career. She made Hollywood history by selling the first Israeli television show to an American network, opening a new market to bring Israeli stories to a global stage. But far from her homeland, she drifted from who she was. A few months after she moved to America, her family called to say *Shanah tovah.* They wanted to wish her a happy Jewish New Year. Noa was startled. She'd forgotten all about the Rosh HaShanah holiday.

That moment pushed Noa to figure out who she was, and as she learned about herself, she learned how misunderstood she was by others – as an Israeli and as a Jew. Noa decided to rededicate herself to supporting her people and country. She had the early foresight to recognize the dangers of online incitement against Israel and helped establish Israel's approach to digital *hasbarah* in an effort to explain and share the truth.

Noa also wrote best-selling books about Israel and the Jewish people to tell their stories to the world. Thanks to these efforts, Noa was appointed Israel's first special envoy for combating antisemitism and delegitimization, fighting public attacks on Israel, much like her own grandfather. Noa was destined to be a storyteller. As an activist, she's not just telling the story. She's changing the plot by fighting to ensure a bright Jewish future.

"I simply couldn't stay silent. I knew there was something else, something deeper."

LEGEND SINCE
1948

OFEK RISHON

TWENTY-FIRST CENTURY | BORN 2005 | ISRAEL

Antibullying Activist

"I want to disappear from the world," Ofek said. Her face was red from sobbing. She reached for yet another tissue, but it all felt pointless. The tears kept flowing. She felt so sad and alone.

From first through sixth grade, Ofek endured relentless bullying. Sometimes, the abuse was verbal. "I donated my hair to cancer patients and had dozens of centimeters cut off. I expected encouragement, but when I posted photos, everyone laughed at me," she recalled. The abuse was also physical. "Once, a boy hit me so hard that when I tried to stop the fall, I landed on my hand and broke it."

When her parents approached the school, they did little to help. "My mother sat all day with counselors and teachers. Every time, they told her that the problem was me," Ofek said. "They threw her the phone numbers of therapists."

At thirteen, Ofek bravely shared her story in a video on social media. When the clip unexpectedly went viral, her painful experience launched a movement to help other bullied kids. With the help of the Israeli TV show *Zinor*, she established the Bully Patrol, a group for victims of bullying. The group expanded quickly and drew attention across Israel to the problem of bullying.

Ofek became a voice for those suffering in silence. She met with politicians and lectured at schools and youth groups. She sat with victims and listened to their stories. "You are loved," she reminded them. "How lucky anyone would be to have you as a friend."

For her efforts, Ofek was honored as one of the top citizens of Israel to light a torch at the official **Yom HaAtzma'ut** national ceremony in celebration of her country's seventy-fifth Independence Day. Her torch lit up the night for all to see, just as she had illuminated a path for many lost in the shadows of bullying.

"Do not let anyone extinguish the fire that burns inside you."

POLGAR SISTERS

TWENTIETH CENTURY | BORN 1960s–1970s | HUNGARY
Chess Champions

The Polgar sisters had an unusual childhood. Their father, Laszlo, believed that "geniuses" were made and not born. Inspired by his brilliant grandfather, who studied Torah in **yeshivah** for several hours a day from age four, Laszlo believed that if children focused on one pursuit from an early age, they could reach the top of their field.

When his oldest daughter expressed an interest in chess, he immersed all three of his girls in a strict training regimen. In the morning, Susan, Sophia, and Judit played sports to build their endurance for long matches. They studied chess the rest of the day and competed at the local park. "We used our winnings on fruit," the girls recalled.

The sisters grew up in a tiny apartment in communist Hungary with limited freedom and few opportunities. Like most families, the Polgars were poor. While some criticized the Polgars' parenting, the sisters appreciated their parents' efforts to find them a path to a better life. "We had nothing," Judit recalled. "They gave us everything."

For the Polgars, chess was more than an experiment in parenting. In a country where anti-Jewish sentiments lurked under the surface, their success in chess helped protect the proudly Jewish family against intimidation. And if needed, they could take the game with them. "Chess uses only the mind and is easy to carry," said Judit. "It suits the constant wanderings of Jewish history."

The sisters worked hard and reached the top of the sport. Susan, the oldest, became the top-ranked female chess player in the world and the third woman ever awarded the title of Grandmaster, the highest honor in chess. The middle sister, Sofia, won multiple medals for Hungary in the Chess Olympics. And the youngest sister, Judit, became, at the time, the youngest Grandmaster – male or female – ever at fifteen. Together, the Polgar sisters are known as the best chess-playing siblings in history.

"Chess is a language that connects us.
Try it and see where it leads you!"
– Judit Polgar

THE PRINTERS

MEDIEVAL ERA | LATE 1400s | ITALY & AROUND THE WORLD
Press Pioneers

For many years, books were copied by hand, but when Johannes Gutenberg invented the printing press, his machine changed everything. As the loud clanging of the metal press replaced the whisper-like strokes of the quill across parchment, the printing press mass-produced books and spread knowledge around the world. At the dawn of this revolution, Jewish women were leaders in the printing and production of Hebrew books.

Estellina Conat, an Italian Jew from Mantua, was likely the very first woman in printing. She operated a printing press with her husband for Hebrew texts and religious books, and printed books on her own account, including the book *Behinat Olam*, written by an important medieval Jewish philosopher. This book was the first inscribed by any female typographer. It is even possible that another Italian Jewish woman was printing one year earlier. Historians debate whether Devorah Cusi oversaw the production of the second-ever printed Hebrew book, a four-volume collection of Jewish laws called the *Tur*. The first Hebrew book was printed by Johannes Gutenberg himself!

As printing spread, Jewish women across Europe became leaders in the publication and distribution of Jewish books. In the Polish city of Lvov, Judith Rosanes was the first Jewish woman to establish a commercial Hebrew press, employing twenty-four men in her business. A true entrepreneur, she charged writers money to produce their books and printed only books she believed would sell. Devorah Romm's press printed thousands of books in Lithuania, including the first printing of the *Vilna Shas*, a printed edition of the Talmud still in use today.

Jewish women printed, even when it was hard. In Spain, the four daughters of Juan de Lucena were charged with the "crime" of printing Hebrew books during the Inquisition. In Constantinople, Doña Reyna Mendes, daughter of Doña Gracia Nasi, was the first Jewish woman to establish her own printing press, and she did it as a Jewish **converso** who converted to Christianity but practiced Judaism in secret – at great risk to her own life. Jewish female printers kept the chain of Jewish tradition unbroken, even when the forces of history tried to tear it apart.

"I, Estellina, the wife of my worthy husband Abraham Conat, wrote this book…"
– Inscription in Behinat Olam

RACHEL

Matriarch

As a girl, Rachel spent hours walking the fertile plains of Haran as she tended her father's flock of sheep. She loved caring for the animals and dreamed of one day being a mother to her own children.

One day, a man named Jacob arrived in Haran. He fell in love with Rachel and agreed to work seven years for her father so he could marry her. Rachel thought she would finally be a mother. But, after being tricked by Rachel's father into marrying her sister, Leah, Jacob agreed to work seven more years for the chance to marry Rachel, and Rachel would have to wait longer to start her family.

Once married, though, Rachel could not become pregnant. Her sadness was overwhelming. "Give me children, or I will die!" Rachel said. Eventually, God remembered Rachel, and she had a son, Joseph. Later, she would give birth to a second son, Benjamin, but, as was sadly common in her time, she died just as he was born.

And yet, in her death, Rachel did not go silent. In the book of Jeremiah in *Nevi'im*, the section of the Tanakh for stories of the prophets, we learn that God heard Rachel crying from up high, wailing and weeping for her children and all the people of Israel.

Jeremiah teaches that when Rachel's descendants were oppressed and enslaved in Egypt, her spirit wept for them, crying as only a mother could, for she felt every sorrow and heard every sigh. Rachel pleaded for hope, mercy, and a safe return to their beloved home, and her prayers were answered. "They shall return from the enemy's land," God declared.

Today, Rachel is the **Ima** of every Jew and is known as Rachel Imeinu, our mother Rachel. She has never stopped caring for her children, throughout the generations.

"Thus said God, 'A cry is heard in Ramah. Wailing, bitter weeping. Rachel weeping for her children.'"
– Jeremiah 31:15

RACHEL EDRI

TWENTIETH CENTURY | BORN 1959 | ISRAEL

Cookie Warrior

October 7, 2023, was supposed to be a joyous day. Rachel was excited to celebrate her husband's sixty-eighth birthday with her children and granddaughters at their home in the southern Israeli town of Ofakim.

But the celebration was not to be. Early that morning, the Hamas leaders who ruled the Gaza Strip, not far from Rachel's home, began firing rockets all over Israel, including into Ofakim. Rachel and her husband ran to a public bomb shelter to protect themselves. While they were spared injury by the rockets, they faced an even greater danger once they returned home, and five armed terrorists burst through the windows.

Though very afraid, Rachel was determined to survive. To save herself and her husband, Rachel decided to treat the violent intruders as though they were any other guests in her home. Rachel asked the men, "Did you eat? Would you like a coffee or tea? I will make it for you." She understood that keeping the terrorists calm would lessen their hostility. "I knew that if they are hungry, they are angry," she explained. For hours, Rachel gave them her husband's birthday cookies, engaged them in conversation, sang them Arabic songs, and tended to their injuries. "One of the terrorists was hurt. I bandaged his wounds and stroked his hand."

While distracting the terrorists with her hospitality and kindness, Rachel was also secretly communicating with the Israeli police outside, using hand signals to inform them of the number of terrorists holding her hostage. Thanks to her help, Israeli special forces, guided by her son, a policeman, eventually entered their home through the roof and rescued Rachel and her husband.

Armed with nothing more than cookies, tea, and quick thinking, Rachel and her story offered a glimmer of light on that dark day. Rachel became famous across Israel as the Cookie **Savta**, or Cookie Grandma. She called on Jewish women to light *Shabbat* candles to remind us of the incredible strength that burns bright in each of us.

"Anyone who is hungry is not in a good mood."

RACHEL "RUCHIE" FREIER

TWENTIETH CENTURY | BORN 1965 | UNITED STATES
Hasidic Judge

The stack of files on Ruchie's desk never seemed to get shorter. She worked as a secretary at a demanding New York law firm. It was a good job. At that time, her husband was learning at a kollel for advanced Torah studies. As a **hasidic** woman, she was proud to support the family to enable her husband to focus on his studies. But the paperwork was nonstop, and the lawyers she worked for were younger than her. *I could do the job they're doing*, she thought. Ruchie left her job and went to college. She dreamed that one day she would be a lawyer, too.

It took ten years, but at the age of forty, Ruchie graduated from law school. At a time when many lawyers were reaching the peak of their careers, Ruchie started at the bottom. She opened an estate law practice and got to work for her community, creating organizations to aid poor families and at-risk youth. She also used her legal know-how and training as a paramedic to create Ezras Nashim, providing emergency ambulance care by women for women.

Ruchie loved public service and considered running for civil court judge. She approached her *rebbetzin*, the rabbi's wife, for approval, who replied without hesitation, "If we can have Deborah the Judge, so too we can have Ruchie." With this meaningful reference to the only female judge in the Hebrew bible, Ruchie launched her campaign.

Her children lined the streets and called out, "Vote for Freier! *S'iz mein mameh*!" Yiddish for "She's my mother!" Her sons hung her campaign signs in the synagogue, and not just on the outside. "Mameh, we're going to put them where the men read – in the bathrooms!" they told her.

Ruchie was elected to the New York Civil Court and, later, to the New York Supreme Court. She became the first hasidic Jewish woman to fill these prestigious seats and the first to hold public office in American history.

"My commitment to the public, my community, and religion go hand in hand."

REBECCA

ANCIENT ISRAEL ERA | MESOPOTAMIA
Matriarch

Her father and brother were wicked, but Rebecca was a righteous woman who emerged from their midst. According to **Midrash**, she was like a "lily among the thorns." So, we can understand why Rebecca chose to break free from her past and chart a new path that changed her life and the future of the Jewish people.

Rebecca's story begins at a well, where she encounters a servant of Abraham seeking a wife for his master's son Isaac. Rebecca offered him water and, without being asked, hurried to provide water for his camels. The servant knew Rebecca was special.

He offered gifts and spoke of the values Abraham's family embraced. The servant proposed the idea of marriage to Rebecca's family. "I will go," she announced, of her own free choice and with deep faith in God. She was ready to leave her home for a new life.

Later, Rebecca became pregnant with twins. Before they were born, God told her they would grow to be two nations, and the older one would serve his younger brother. As the twin boys grew up, it became clear that they were very different. The older son, Esau, was an outdoorsman and a hunter, and Jacob, the younger son, was a man of peace. Despite the custom at the time for the firstborn son to receive his father's blessing and lead the next generation, Rebecca knew this was not God's will.

Driven by foresight and divine purpose, Rebecca orchestrated a clever plan for the younger son, Jacob, to receive his father's blessing instead of his older brother. "My son, listen carefully as I instruct you," Rebecca told Jacob. "Do as I say." When the plan succeeded, she helped Jacob escape from the angry Esau and saved his life.

With her decisive actions, Rebecca enforced God's will. She ensured that Jacob would become the next leader of the Jewish people and that they would forever be known by the name God would soon give him: Israel.

"I will go."
– Genesis 24:58

RIVKA RAVITZ

TWENTIETH CENTURY | BORN 1976 | ISRAEL
Chief of Staff

Rivka was excited about a career in teaching but soon realized that the salary was hardly enough to support her growing family. She was an ultra-Orthodox **haredi** woman and, like most women in her community, hoped to be blessed with many children. Her father-in-law, a Knesset member in Israel's parliament and leader of the Finance Committee, needed an assistant. She applied for the position and was accepted.

Rivka's early days in the Knesset were overwhelming. "It seemed so big," she said. "I had to learn how a budget worked." She took piles of paper home, studying them all night to prepare for meetings the next day. Soon, the Knesset became her second home.

When a new law prevented Knesset officials from hiring family, Rivka went to work for another member of the Finance Committee, Reuven Rivlin. Now highly experienced, Rivka was promoted to bureau chief and played a vital role in his campaigns for speaker of the Knesset and, later, his successful bid for Israel's presidency. When Rivlin became the president of Israel, Rivka was named his chief of staff. She managed his team and all of his official activities.

Rivka accompanied President Rivlin to important meetings, including at the White House. When US President Joe Biden learned that Rivka was a mother of twelve and an accomplished civil servant, he knelt admiringly before her on one knee.

Even while working demanding hours and traveling frequently for state visits, Rivka maintained the practices of Jewish law and embraced her role as an opportunity to fulfill the mitzvah of *kiddush Hashem*, making God's name holy.

She also never forgot the holy work of teachers, and as soon as she got the chance, raised a fight for teachers' salaries in the state budget.

"People respect you when you respect your beliefs."

ROSALIE SILBERMAN ABELLA

TWENTIETH CENTURY | BORN 1946 | CANADA

Supreme Court Justice

The Silbermans were married just as the Nazis invaded Poland. They chose life in the face of fear and soon had a son, but the family was deported to the concentration camps. The parents managed to survive. Their young son did not.

After the war, they decided to choose life again and start their family anew. They had a daughter and then another. Little Rosalie was born in a displaced persons camp in Germany, and when she was four, the Silbermans immigrated to Canada with little more than hope for a better future.

Rosalie's father had trained as a lawyer in Europe and even defended displaced persons in the camps. He hoped to practice law in Canada but was told he could not. You had to be a citizen, and he wasn't.

When he came home and told the family the news, Little Rosalie spoke up. "If you can't be a lawyer, then I'm going to be a lawyer!" She wasn't sure what that meant but was taught that anything was possible with hard work.

Rosalie worked hard and, after graduating from law school, was appointed a family court judge. She was the first Jewish female judge in Canada and the youngest in the country's history. Many of the Jewish men she worked with changed their names to conceal their Jewish identity, but Rosalie never did. "I wanted people to know who I was. I would succeed on hard work alone. I had **chutzpah**!" she said.

In her career, Rosalie worked tirelessly to eliminate the disadvantages faced by people with disabilities, women, people of color, and the native aboriginal community. After twenty-five years as a champion of human rights and equality, Justice Rosie became the first Jewish woman to sit on the Supreme Court of Canada.

"We have to wear our identities with pride."

ROSALYN YALOW

TWENTIETH CENTURY | BORN 1921 | UNITED STATES

Medical Physicist

More than half a billion people in the world are living with diabetes, and many of them would not be alive today if it weren't for Rosalyn. Diabetes is a disease that occurs when your blood sugar is too high due to the lack of a hormone called insulin. When your blood sugar is out of control, it can lead to dangerous complications. To test whether someone has diabetes, a doctor needs to know how much insulin is in the blood. The problem is that insulin is extremely small. How can you know the level of insulin when you can't see it?

Rosalyn created a method called radioimmunoassay. To check if someone has diabetes, she used glowing radioactive insulin like a flashlight to accurately detect the amount of insulin in the blood. Rosalyn's method changed the lives of people with diabetes, thyroid disease, growth issues, and fertility challenges. It revolutionized endocrinology and other areas of medicine, earning her a Nobel Prize in Medicine, the top award in her field. Thanks to Rosalyn's discovery, people living with diabetes can receive the appropriate medicine and treatments they need to stay healthy and alive.

This achievement was especially remarkable given the challenges that Rosalyn had to overcome as a Jew and a woman. While pursuing her studies, one school rejected her because they had a **quota** for the number of Jewish students they would admit each year. Later, she was the only woman permitted to teach at a university with over four hundred male professors.

Rosalyn also changed the way people thought about women scientists. Many felt women had to choose between pursuing scientific work and raising a family. Rosalyn believed that women could do both. Being a Jewish wife and mother was just as important to her as her lab achievements. She kept a kosher home, invited her colleagues over for Passover Seders, and worried about them when they got sick. If they also gave Nobel Prizes for being a mom, Rosalyn may have won that too!

"I have my marriage and two wonderful children. I have a laboratory that is an absolute joy. I have health. As long as there is something to do, I am happy."

ROSE SCHNEIDERMAN

EMANCIPATION ERA | BORN 1882 | UNITED STATES
Trade Unionist

In minutes, the flames raced through the factory, fueled by fabric scraps and paper patterns strewn about the floor. With many of the exits locked, the workers, mostly young immigrant girls, were trapped inside. Nearly 150 died in the Triangle Shirtwaist Factory fire, one of the worst workplace disasters in American history.

Many were shocked by the tragedy, but not Rose. These were the terrible workplace conditions that she was fighting to change. "Every week, I must learn of the untimely death of one of my sister workers," Rose cried out. She was a labor organizer with the New York Women's Trade Union League and would soon be its national president.

Rose was born to a religious family in Poland. Both her parents worked in sewing. Not long after her family emigrated to America and settled in the **tenements** of New York's Lower East Side, her father died, and the family fell into poverty. Rose left school at thirteen and started working as a lining stitcher in a cap factory.

After laboring in uncomfortable and dangerous work conditions, she organized the women working in the factory and established the first labor union to advocate for their rights. When the city's cap makers went on strike, Rose was elected to represent their demands and quickly attained prominence as a powerful speaker and one of the toughest labor leaders in America. She later served as labor advisor to President Franklin D. Roosevelt.

Rose was instrumental in the fight for an eight-hour workday, minimum wage laws, and women's right to vote. She famously argued, "The worker must have bread, but she must have roses, too." Rose believed that everyone should have more than just the means to live but the means to enjoy a life worth living.

> *"What the woman who labors wants is the right to live, not simply exist."*

ROTHSCHILD WOMEN

Political Strategists

For two thousand years, Jews felt as if they were living in a long, dark tunnel. Lost in the Diaspora, fleeing one foreign land for another, each generation wept over their expulsion from the Jewish homeland and longed one day to return.

From this blackness emerged the dream of Zionism, a movement to create a state for the Jewish people in the Land of Israel. After World War I, this land was under the control of the British. The Zionist leaders knew that to escape the tunnel, they would need the support of the British government for a Jewish state, and to get its support, they would need the help of Britain's most powerful Jewish family, the Rothschilds.

The Rothschilds were not supporters of Zionism. For many years, they had helped Eastern European Jewish immigrants blend into British society, leaving behind their old traditions and languages. The Rothschilds were worried that a Jewish state would disrupt these efforts, but nineteen-year-old Dorothy Rothschild, a new addition to the family through marriage, began a correspondence with Zionist leader Chaim Weizmann. They discussed the realities of antisemitism and the need for a safe haven for the Jews.

Dorothy enlisted two more Rothschild women, Rózsika and Peggy. They helped advance the Zionist cause within the hallways of British power, building important alliances that changed British attitudes toward Zionism. They gave Weizmann a diplomatic makeover, refining his gruff manner to better resonate with conservative British society.

Finally, a ray of light cracked through the tunnel. The British foreign secretary, Arthur Balfour, wrote a letter announcing the British government's support for the creation of a home for the Jewish people in their ancient land. The **Balfour Declaration** was addressed to Walter Rothschild, the male head of the family, but it was the Rothschild women who were its undeclared champions.

> *"I love fanatics and idealists.*
> *Chaim Weizmann is both."*
> *– Rózsika Rothschild*

Foreign Office,
November 2nd, 1917.

Dear Lord Rothschild,

I have much pleasure in conveying to you, on behalf of His Majesty's Government, the following declaration of symp... ...onist aspirations which has been s... ...by, the

...r th...

...eclar...
...te...

ROYA HAKAKIAN

TWENTIETH CENTURY | BORN 1966 | IRAN
Writer-Journalist

When the Second Holy Temple in Jerusalem was destroyed, a group of Jews fled to Persia. In the **Persian** city of Shushan, a Jewish woman named Esther became queen. When Jews celebrate Purim each year, they read the story of how she saved her people from near destruction. Jews have lived there ever since.

Hundreds of years later, Persia became the country of Iran. There, another Jewish girl, Roya, grew up in the capital city. When she was thirteen, her country and her life changed dramatically when a new group of religious Muslim leaders overthrew the Iranian leader and came to power determined to rule according to strict religious principles.

The new government forced women to cover their hair and wear loose-fitting clothing so only their faces and hands could be seen. Women were banned from many jobs and were not allowed to be in some public spaces. Along with the new rules for women, Roya and the Persian Jews also felt threatened by increasing antisemitism and violence. As a teen, Roya found comfort in writing and began to publish her poems.

Eventually, Roya and her family fled Iran for safety and freedom in the United States. Finding her voice and writing in a new language took time, but she worked hard and spoke out about her experience in Iran, being forced to leave and not having the freedom to read, write, and say what she wanted.

Today, Roya is a celebrated writer and has published several books, including a memoir called *Journey from the Land of No,* about her childhood in revolutionary Iran. After losing and then regaining her freedom as a woman and a Jew, Roya now lives in a world of *yes* and embraces the value of free expression. "Judaism fosters free-thinking and individuality," said Roya. "This is too rare in the world today." Like Queen Esther, she uses her voice to speak her mind and save innocent people from injustice.

"The space to think freely is the greatest gift."

RUDOLPHINA MENZEL

EMANCIPATION ERA | BORN 1891 | AUSTRIA

Cynologist

A dog nipped Rudolphina when she was only four, but it was love at first bite. She became the dog rescuer of her Vienna neighborhood, and when her parents refused to house all twenty of her growing pack, she paid neighbors to take them in.

Once a hobby, Rudolphina's passion turned into a profession. After earning a doctorate in science, she conducted groundbreaking research on dog behavior, proving that dogs could detect individual human scents. She started a dog ranch and trained them to provide security, assisting Austrian police and military agencies.

Rudolphina's love of dogs was matched only by her love of Zionism, the belief in a home for Jews in their historic land. As it was common to train security dogs in a foreign language so criminals could not redirect them, she taught her dogs to obey commands in Hebrew.

When the Nazis took control of Austria and life became unsafe for Jews, Rudolphina fled with forged papers to what was then British Mandate Palestine, leaving hundreds of dogs behind. Many of these dogs were used by the Nazi army. Ironically, they only obeyed Hebrew, so the Nazis would have had to use Hebrew commands.

In the *Yishuv*, Rudolphina got to work training dogs to protect the early Jewish communities of the future State of Israel by patrolling the land and detecting intruders. She helped create the canine unit of the **Haganah**, which later became the renowned *Oketz* unit of the Israeli army. During Israel's War of Independence, these dogs transported messages, detected explosives, and carried supplies. When Israel won the war, her four-legged warriors marched through Tel Aviv's streets in victory parades.

At the end of her career, Rudolphina trained seeing-eye dogs to support the mobility of people with visual disabilities and established the first guide-dog center in the Middle East. In war and peace, Rudolphina and her dogs never stopped serving others.

"Dogs built the country no less than the plow, tractor, gun, and water tower."

RUTH & NAOMI

Royal Matriarchs

The ground cracked under the unyielding heat. A devastating famine gripped the land of Judea. Naomi, her husband Elimelech, and their two sons left their home and fled to the country of Moab. Sadly, Elimelech soon passed away. Naomi's two sons married local Moabite women, Orpah and Ruth, but within a few years, her sons passed away, too.

Naomi heard that the fields of Judea were blooming again and decided to return home. She urged her beloved daughters-in-law Orpah and Ruth to rebuild their lives in Moab. Naomi kissed them goodbye and cried out through flowing tears. "Turn back, my daughters! Why should you go with me?"

Orpah decided to stay in Moab, but Ruth clung to Naomi. "Where you go, I will go. Where you stay, I will stay. Your people shall be my people, and your God my God," said Ruth. When Naomi saw how determined she was to go with her, she stopped arguing. According to the Rabbis, Ruth **converted** and became a Jew.

Naomi and Ruth arrived in Judea at the beginning of the barley harvest. Ruth set off to glean barley from the fields to provide for her mother-in-law. As luck would have it, the fields belonged to Boaz, a relative of Elimelech. Astonished by Ruth's loyalty to Naomi, Boaz offered her water, food, protection, and blessings.

With Naomi's encouragement, Ruth pursued Boaz, married him, and soon gave birth to a son named Oved. Naomi picked up the infant and held him to her chest, her soul renewed after many years of sorrow. She would be like a mother to the child.

That baby would grow up to become the grandfather of the mighty King David. It is believed that one day, a Messiah will come who will gather the Jewish people back to the Land of Israel and bring peace to the world. This Messiah will descend from King David and his great-grandmother, the loyal and devoted daughter-in-law Ruth.

"Where you go, I will go."
– Ruth 1:16

RUTH BADER GINSBURG

TWENTIETH CENTURY | BORN 1933 | UNITED STATES
Supreme Court Justice

At an early age, Ruth experienced the sting of inequality. While at a cousin's bar mitzvah, the ancient rite of passage for thirteen-year-old boys entering Jewish adulthood, Ruth wondered why there wasn't a similar ceremony for Jewish girls like her. In the traditional community in which she was raised, bat mitzvahs weren't celebrated at that time. So, when Ruth reached the same age, she raised her voice and published a letter in her synagogue newsletter urging every congregant to fight injustice.

Ruth would continue fighting injustice at every level of society. She excelled in her studies and went on to law school. Ruth was one of only nine women in a class of five hundred men. Despite being a top student, the head of the law school once asked her, "Why are you taking the place of a man?" Ginsburg brushed off the comment and graduated at the top of her class.

Because she was a woman and a Jew, no law firm would hire her. So, Ruth became a professor and volunteered for an organization seeking equal treatment for all. Ruth won important court cases, became a judge, and eventually was appointed by the president of the United States to be only the second woman and the first Jewish woman to serve as a justice on the US Supreme Court, the nation's highest and most important court. She was known as a fierce champion of equality. In her later years, she was nicknamed "Notorious RBG" for her willingness to fight for her beliefs, even if they were not the court's majority opinion.

Ruth became famous for her deep commitment to the Jewish value of **tzedek**. Inspired by the humanity and bravery of her role models, Emma Lazarus and Henrietta Szold, Ruth worked tirelessly to follow the ancient command from the Torah, "*Tzedek, tzedek tirdof*," meaning, "Justice, justice shall you pursue." She even had the words painted on the walls of her office and hung a large silver mezuzah on the doorpost to always remember who she was and what she stood for. Ruth believed that being a Jew and a judge just "fit together." The pursuit of justice, she said, runs through the entirety of Jewish history and Jewish tradition.

"I am a judge, born, raised, and proud of being a Jew."

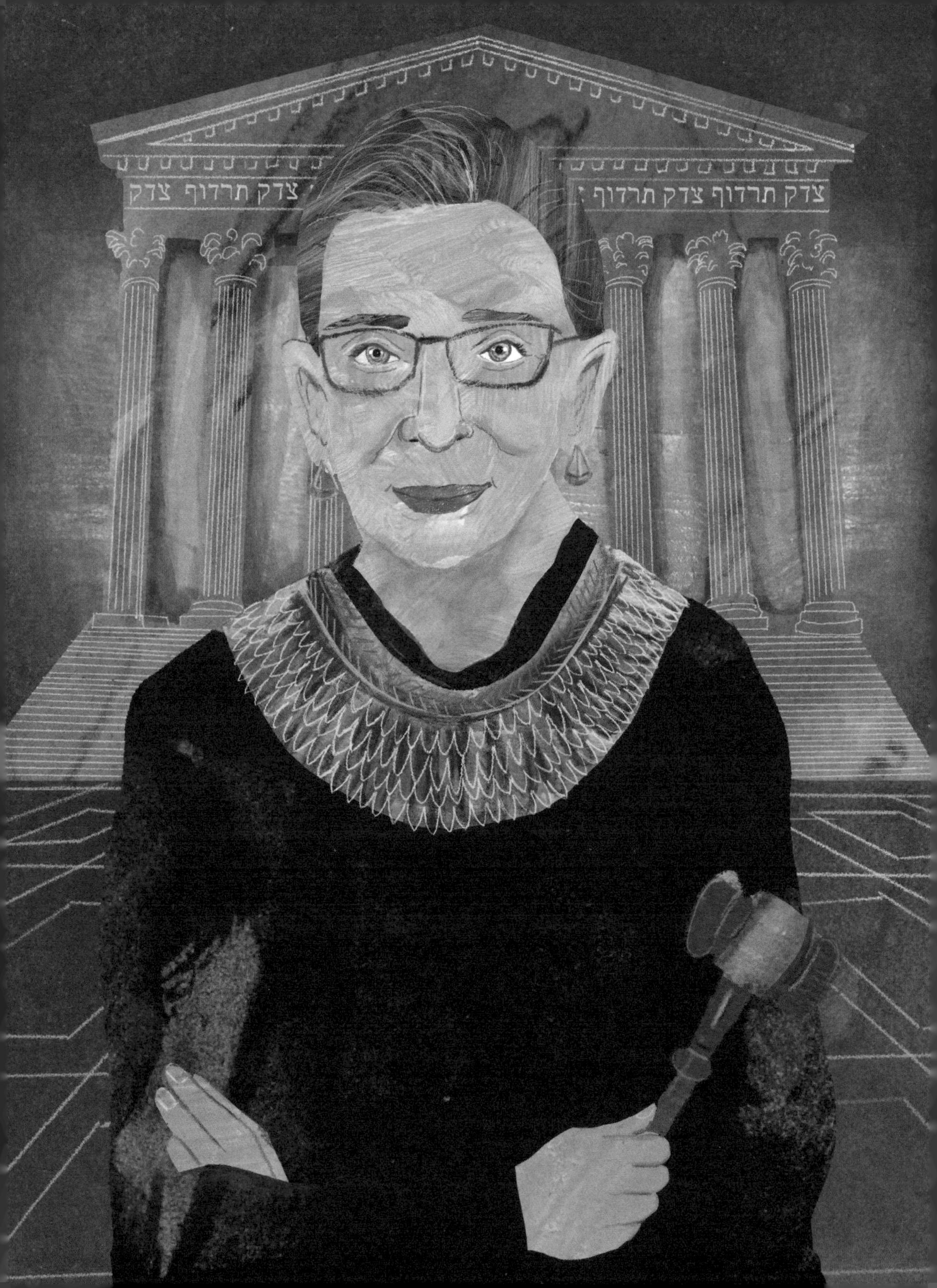
צדק תרדוף צדק
צדק תרדוף צדק תרדוף

RUTH DREIFUSS

TWENTIETH CENTURY | BORN 1940 | SWITZERLAND

National President

Turn your head, and you might just miss her walking briskly through the halls of government. She won't be wearing a designer suit and towering heels. She'll be toting her own black briefcase and wearing sensible flat shoes. After all, the cobblestone streets in the capital city of Bern can get very slippery when it snows. Ruth will look like any commuter on her way to work, except she's not. Ruth is one of the most important people in all of Switzerland.

She was born in the historic village of St. Gallen to an old Swiss Jewish family, but fears of a **Nazi** invasion during World War II led her family to flee, eventually resettling in the city of Geneva. All the while, her family aided Jewish refugees secretly entering the country, even at risk to their own lives.

As Ruth got older, she wanted to devote her life to service. She got involved in politics, advocating tirelessly for the rights of workers and women, first as the head of Switzerland's labor unions and later as minister for domestic affairs.

Despite strong opposition, she fought for paid maternity leave to allow women to support their families while caring for their babies at home. She prompted Switzerland to confront its own role in the injustices of World War II, the very war that displaced her family and devastated millions of others.

Ruth broke two glass ceilings when she became the first woman *and* the first Jew to serve as Switzerland's president. Ruth didn't want people to fuss over her with flowers or treat her like a shiny piece of jewelry. She wanted to get to work. And she did, with her trademark no-nonsense resolve. As Ruth knows, you don't have to be flashy to blaze a trail.

"I don't want to be treated, bouquets of flowers and all, as though I were only a piece of jewelry."

RUTH HANDLER & ELLIE GOLDSTEIN

TWENTIETH CENTURY | BORN 1916   TWENTY-FIRST CENTURY | BORN 2001
UNITED STATES   UNITED KINGDOM

Inventor & Model

Ruth shifted uncomfortably as she watched her children, Kenneth and Barbara, play in the living room. Kenneth rowdily amused himself with toy trucks and soldiers. Barbara quietly nursed her baby dolls.

Ruth was the tenth child of poor Polish immigrants and had to work jobs from a young age. She didn't like how the baby dolls reinforced the narrow notion that little girls should grow up only to be housewives and mothers. She wanted to create a toy that would empower girls to believe they could do and be anything they wanted.

Ruth created Barbie, naming the toy after her daughter. The adult-shaped doll allowed girls to act out their imagined futures in proudly girl-centric make-believe scenes. A few years later, she launched a male doll named Ken, after her son, but he got second billing. In Barbie's world, women took center stage.

Some criticized Barbie for presenting an unrealistic body image with impossibly long legs and a tiny waist, but there was no denying her popularity. At a time when opportunities for girls were limited, Barbie was revolutionary. She had hundreds of careers, from astronomer to zoologist. As a Jewish woman who experienced antisemitism, Ruth wanted Barbie to encourage young girls to love and accept all people, regardless of differences. The dolls were produced in different skin tones. One of Barbie's friends was a black doll named Christie.

Barbie continues to promote **tolerance** and acceptance to this day. Nearly sixty-five years after the first Barbie, a Jewish girl named Ellie made history by helping to launch a Barbie with the genetic condition Down's syndrome. Ellie, the first model with Down's syndrome to appear on the covers of top fashion magazines, loves the new doll. "She's glamorous, gorgeous, and darling," Ellie said. "She is perfect like me, and I am perfect like her."

*"Barbie represents the fact
that a woman has choices."
– Ruth Handler*

SARAH

ANCIENT ISRAEL ERA | MESOPOTAMIA
Matriarch

Sarah left behind her home and family for the distant land of Canaan, buoyed by the promise of children.

One day, God would bless her husband Abraham with descendants as numerous as the stars. But as the years turned into decades, Sarah's hope faded into quiet resignation. She was ninety years old, withering and barren. Sarah's faith was strong, but in her old age, God's promise felt as distant as the stars themselves.

One day, three strangers appeared under a tree, bringing with them a message from God. As Abraham spoke with the visitors inside his tent, Sarah lingered at the entrance, a spark of curiosity gleaming in her aged eyes. Then, she overheard the news that defied nature and time – she would bear a son within the year.

At that moment, Sarah laughed within herself, not believing that she would have a baby at her late age. The commentator **Rashi** wrote that she was filled with questions. Could her womb even bear a child? It seemed impossible. Yet, within that laugh, within the questions, something stirred – a flicker of hope reignited, the joy of new possibilities, a daring to believe in the unbelievable.

God heard her laughter and asked Abraham, "Why did Sarah laugh?" Out of fear, Sarah denied it, but she couldn't hide her feelings from God. The laughter was her response to the possibility of her deepest desire coming to life against all odds.

Sarah became the first Jewish mother and gave birth to a son named Isaac. His name meant laughter in Hebrew, and his descendants would be as numerous as the stars of heaven. Sarah had the courage to laugh in the face of difficulty and trust in God, even when hope felt as far away as a distant star.

"God has brought me laughter."
– Genesis 21:6

SARAH SCHENIRER

EMANCIPATION ERA | BORN 1883 | POLAND

Education Activist

It was **Rosh HaShanah**, the holiest day on the Jewish calendar, but for Sarah, the New Year festival felt hollow.

The fathers and sons of her community were off visiting the great Polish hasidic rebbes in the towns of Ger and Belz, leaving the wives, daughters, and little ones at home in the capital city of Kraków. At synagogue, Sarah could barely hear the prayers in the walled-off women's section. Most of her friends stayed outside and played games, seemingly unaware of the day's importance.

At a young age, Sarah earned the nickname Little Hasid. She had strong faith in God at a time when many women of her generation were losing faith altogether. She loved learning Torah and was jealous of the opportunities her brothers had. While they could continue their Torah study in yeshivah after elementary school, she had to become a seamstress.

When World War I broke out, Sarah fled Poland for nearby Austria. At a synagogue in Vienna, she heard a powerful sermon describing the role of women throughout Jewish history. She decided then to do all she could to rekindle faith in Judaism by providing Orthodox religious girls a strong education. With a blessing from important spiritual leaders, the Gerrer Rebbe and the Belzer Rebbe, Sarah started a school for twenty-five girls in her sewing studio.

The Bais Yaakov school integrated a love for Torah and mitzvot with secular knowledge, honoring the rich heritage of Judaism while embracing modern education. Over time and long after Sarah's life, Bais Yaakov became a worldwide movement, with hundreds of schools worldwide, from Jerusalem to Johannesburg.

Sarah never had children, but thousands of Bais Yaakov students still honor her today with the loving nickname Sarah Imeinu, our mother Sarah, just like her namesake in the Torah, the first Jewish woman.

"My dear girls, the destiny of Israel is in your hands."

SHEYNA GIFFORD

TWENTIETH CENTURY | BORN 1973 | UNITED STATES

Space Doctor

Sheyna always dreamed of going to Mars. She pulled on her space helmet and looked out over the volcanic expanse. Her new home looked just like the real thing. Mounds of rust-red rock and hardened lava encrusted the landscape. Sheyna couldn't wait to explore. She switched her radio on, opened the airlock door, and set off.

As a crew member on a year-long simulated Mars mission on a remote slope of Mauna Loa volcano in Hawaii, Sheyna was pursuing her childhood dream of becoming an astronaut. In university, she studied astrophysics, a common area of study for aspiring space voyagers, but when several loved ones got sick, Sheyna's interests expanded to the health sciences as well. She decided to take a different orbit to the stars – as a space doctor.

On NASA's HI-SEAS IV simulated Mars mission, Sheyna and her five crew members lived inside a small fiberglass dome, grew their own fresh food, and wore spacesuits when they ventured outside. The purpose of the mission was to study how humans can live and work together during long-duration space missions, like those that might be needed for a future trip to Mars.

As crew doctor, Sheyna was responsible for monitoring their daily health. With a built-in communications delay to the outside world simulating real-life conditions, Sheyna's responsibility to provide emergency care carried greater risks.

Sheyna continued to live a Jewish life on simulated Mars. On Friday mornings before Shabbat, she baked **challah** using the yeast she had kept alive all week. When dust storms created heating issues in the dome, Sheyna placed the bread culture near her bed to keep it warm.

And while fire wasn't permitted, Sheyna switched on her electric Shabbat candles on Friday nights and thought about the light of millions of Jews throughout history who kept Shabbat even when it seemed impossible. Their courage inspired Sheyna to be part of another seemingly impossible mission: to help humans find a path to Mars and return home healthy.

"Make your life a story worth telling."

SHLOMTZION

Queen

Queen Shlomtzion rose to power at a moment of great uncertainty in the land of Judea. By the time her husband, the Maccabee king Alexander Yannai, had died and made Shlomtzion the queen regent, the once mighty Maccabee army was weak and weary from war. The kingdom was absorbed in conflict between the two largest and most influential Jewish groups of the time, the Sadducees and the Pharisees. Judea was divided and vulnerable to attack.

The Sadducees were an elite group who wanted to keep their special status as priests and adopted Greek customs and ideas. The Pharisees tried to preserve the ways of the Torah through the **Oral Law**. They believed that along with the written Torah, God shared with Moses at Mount Sinai a set of teachings that explain and expand on the written laws.

Shlomtzion threw her support behind the Pharisees and made the Oral Law the law of her court. Under her reign, the Torah was not just a religious text but a living guide, influencing every aspect of life. She expanded the services of the Second Temple in Jerusalem to allow more people to celebrate the holidays and pray to God.

Shlomtzion was also a champion of justice and the welfare of everyone, not just the elite. She established a system of traveling judges to ensure that even the most remote corners of Judea received justice and lived according to the law.

Shlomtzion, whose name in Hebrew means "wholeness of Zion," reminds us that the Jewish people are made whole and united by wisdom, not the sword. Unlike the rulers who came before and after, Shlomtzion chose a path of diplomacy and strengthened Judea from within, ushering in an era of peace and untold prosperity. According to the Talmud, when Shlomtzion was queen, the soil was so rich that grains of wheat grew as large as kidney beans, oats as large as olives, and lentils as large as gold coins.

"She preserved the nation in wholeness."
– Flavius Josephus, historian

SHOSHANA CARDIN

TWENTIETH CENTURY | BORN 1926 | UNITED STATES
Political Activist

In the Golden Age of Hollywood, before smartphones, tablets, and even televisions, children waited all week to see their favorite stars on the big screen. But for Shoshana, the biggest stars weren't in Hollywood. Her heroes were uncelebrated people fighting bravely for what they believed in far corners of the world. While her friends filled cups with popcorn at the Sunday matinee, eleven-year-old Shoshana stood under the flashing bulbs of the marquee sign gilding a popular Baltimore theater to fill jars of coins for the stars of the *Yishuv*, the courageous Jewish pioneers settling the Land of Israel.

Shoshana could have made her name on the big screen. She was an elegant and beautiful woman. She was told she could be a successful model. But Shoshana wanted to work where she could have the greatest impact. She married and became a public school teacher. At that time, pregnant women weren't allowed to teach. When she discovered she was expecting her first child, she stopped teaching and devoted herself to volunteering as a **lay leader** and philanthropist for her local and Jewish communities. Shoshana gave her money and time to help others and make the world better.

Shoshana fearlessly lobbied presidents and prime ministers in pursuit of justice. She helped secure the liberation of over a million Soviet Jews and provided them with the resources to rebuild their lives in Israel. She helped to unite a fractured Jewish world by opposing a divisive law preventing many Jews from becoming citizens of Israel.

Shoshana was the first woman to play a leading role in nearly every major Jewish organization, including the first woman to serve as the president of the vital Jewish Federations of North America. She doesn't have a star on the Hollywood Walk of Fame, but her legacy shines on and will light the way for others for generations to come.

"The most important message I want to give is the pride, responsibility, and blessing of being Jewish. That's what gives me the strength to challenge what I have challenged and bring about change where I could."

JEWISH UNITY IS THREATENED
עם ישרא חי
I AM MY BROTHER'S
שומר אחי אנכי!
העם היהודי
שומר אח
אנכי
עם ישרא חי
JEWISH
עם ישראל חי

SIVAN RAHAV-MEIR

TWENTIETH CENTURY | BORN 1981 | ISRAEL

Journalist

The other kids had cool hobbies, like gymnastics and guitar. Sivan failed at everything she tried until she discovered her unique talents. "I loved writing and I was good at it," she said.

Sivan started interviewing kids in her first-grade class. The girl sitting next to her had recently adopted a dog. Sivan described the story in an article and sent it to a kids' magazine. The article was published! At the age of six, Sivan became a journalist.

Sivan wrote about all thirty-five kids in her class. Soon, she got a call from the biggest news studio in Israel. They'd read her articles and invited her to be a youth reporter. Sivan interviewed famous Israeli politicians, from Yitzhak Rabin to Shimon Peres.

When she was fifteen, Sivan met three **dati** girls. She had interviewed many people but had never met anyone religious. Sivan was curious about their lives, so she decided to interview them. Halfway through, they asked her to stop. "You don't understand us," they said. "Come for Shabbat."

Sivan arrived at their Shabbat table as a journalist but left entirely changed. "It was so inspiring!" She went again and again and started keeping Shabbat too. When Sivan stopped working on Shabbat, her colleagues discouraged her. "This will be an obstacle to your career," they said. It turned out to be a gift. "It changed the way I cover the news," she said. "I can now tell a bigger story."

Today, Sivan is one of the most popular female journalists in Israel. She writes for Israel's largest newspaper, is a television and radio host, and teaches daily about Judaism on social media. "You may not be good at everything," she said. "But find the gift that Hashem gave you."

"What are you good at? Ask yourself, what were you put in this world to do?"

SHULAMIT LEVENBERG

TWENTIETH CENTURY | BORN 1970 | ISRAEL
Biomedical Engineer

The rats were paralyzed from the waist down like the millions of people injured each year in accidents and confined to wheelchairs. While healthy rats can use their front and back legs to walk, the paralyzed rats had damage to their spinal cords, leaving their hind legs useless.

Shulamit and her team implanted a piece of lab-made tissue with stem cells into the damaged part of their spinal cords and inserted tiny, modified exosomes into their noses, spurring the nerve cells to regrow. Exosomes are like little packages that cells use to send messages to each other. Amazingly, many of the rats could soon walk normally again. Shulamit understood this meant that paralyzed people might one day walk again too.

In addition to treating paralysis, Shulamit's research in tissue engineering has led to new treatments for some of today's most serious conditions, such as type 2 diabetes and heart disease. "Many conditions can be treated with engineered tissue," Shulamit said. "Our goal is to provide a cure." She hopes to one day create new organs with a 3D printer that could customize organs like a kidney or a heart to fit a patient's body exactly.

Shulamit's research is also helping people eat better. She created edible cultured meat by bioprinting a plant-based tissue and mixing it with animal cells. This method is now used to make meat in a lab while avoiding the need to kill animals. It also reduces harm to the environment caused by the raising and slaughtering of animals for meat.

Shulamit's innovations have made her one of Israel's leading inventors. She holds patents for innovative technologies and has founded multiple startup companies. Shulamit herself is an observant woman with strong Jewish beliefs. "It is a **mitzvah** to study and better the world," she said. "Understanding the world's complexities brings us closer to our Creator."

"As we look into the future, the opportunities are limitless."

THE SPIRITUAL LEADERS

Religious Pioneers

For millennia, women have held significant roles in religious education, synagogue leadership, the development of Jewish law, and spiritual guidance.

Deborah, the prophetess and judge, provided spiritual and judicial leadership, and Bruriah, a respected Talmudic-era scholar, engaged in important legal debates. Kurdish scholar Asenath Barzani led a yeshivah and was greatly respected for her knowledge, while Hannah Rachel Verbermacher, a rare female hasidic rebbe, led a group of followers and performed religious rituals.

Women in these roles varyingly encountered acceptance and rejection by both traditional and liberal Jewish authorities. Asenath was left out of history books and struggled to receive financial support for her yeshivah. Hannah was told to stop her activities.

Women have also strived for positions of rabbinic leadership. Regina Jonas, who grew up in an Orthodox home in Germany, was the first woman known to publicly express the desire to become a rabbi. In her doctoral thesis, she argued that women should be able to serve as rabbis under the Jewish law. Since no rabbinical body would **ordain** a woman at that time, Regina was ordained by a liberal rabbi in a private ceremony.

Nonetheless, Regina was never offered an official rabbinic position. She instead served as a spiritual counselor at hospitals, prisons, and senior homes. As life worsened for German Jews, she visited communities across the country, but eventually, Regina was deported to a Nazi concentration camp. There, she continued giving spiritual guidance for two more years before she was tragically murdered.

Today, Jewish women are leading in all areas, from the classroom to the boardroom and the house of prayer to the home. Even in traditional Orthodox communities, women are certified to advise individuals on questions of Jewish practice and law. Women continue to strive for greater opportunities to serve in Jewish religious life.

"...the Holy One, Blessed be He, granted a woman a greater understanding [bina] than that of a man."
– Niddah 45b

TEMERL BERGSON

EARLY MODERN ERA | BORN 1764 | POLAND
Philanthropist

Temerl's father was very wealthy, but she was not content to live a life of luxury. She used her resources and influence to champion the causes she believed in, most notably the new hasidic movement in Poland.

Temerl loved being Jewish and wanted every Jew to feel the same. Hasidism was like a cool breeze for a Jewish practice that had grown stuffy with strict rules and study. The movement offered a joyful Judaism filled with singing, dancing, and heartfelt prayer. It emphasized a personal connection with God rather than just intellectual understanding.

Temerl faced many challenges in her life. She was married at a young age and soon widowed. Later, she married again, and her second husband, too, passed away. But Temerl showed strength in difficult times. She successfully led the family business and founded a bank at a time when few women could.

Her business savvy was matched only by her philanthropy. It was said that she donated her money so generously, as though it were as plentiful as ashes. A pillar of the community, she gave to Polish and Jewish causes and built the first hasidic synagogue and **beit midrash**, or house of study, in the area.

In addition to financial support, she also employed hasidic Jews in her business and paid the salaries of its greatest scholars. When Jews faced persecution by Polish authorities, Temerl boldly defended their rights and worked to overturn a law banning the celebration of the Jewish holidays. When Hasidism came under investigation, she cleared its leaders of suspicion and enabled the movement to grow.

'Reb Temerl,' as she was called by many, was a devoted mother to her six children, as well as the mother of the hasidic movement and to future generations of Jews inspired by its joyful song.

"To her nation, she was a protector against oppression – a helper during distress.
To the poor, she was a mother."
– Temerl's gravestone

TRUDE DOTHAN

TWENTIETH CENTURY | BORN 1922 | AUSTRIA
Archaeologist

As a girl, Trude was determined to be an archaeologist. She loved digging in the ground to discover the places and peoples of the past. And she especially loved digging up her own history as a Jew in the Land of Israel.

Trude became an archaeology professor and was passionate about teaching all that she had found. In a course on ancient pottery, she encouraged her students to study and feel the Iron Age pottery materials by tossing pottery sherds around the class. By accident, one fragment hit a student on the forehead!

Years later, Trude and this former student would share a laugh as they dug side by side at an excavation at Tel Miqne. A *tel* is a hill with layers of history buried underneath. There, they unearthed the biblical city of Ekron, mentioned numerous times in **Nevi'im**, the Book of Prophets.

By then, Trude had become a world-renowned archaeologist. In the early years of the State of Israel, she supervised many ground-breaking excavations, including the discovery of ancient Egyptian fortresses and evidence of the many people that had passed through the Land of Israel.

She also led excavations outside Israel. At Atienou in Cyprus, she directed the first archaeological dig conducted by an Israeli team abroad. "I was fascinated by the coexistence of cultures in the region," she said.

When she wasn't digging, Trude gave talks on archaeology worldwide. Once, she spoke before a packed university auditorium. Strangely, the walkways were packed, but the first rows were empty. It seems, the last time she'd taught there, the long pointer stick she excitedly used to note details on the screen accidentally hit the students sitting in these front rows. She may not have had perfect aim, but she was always precise with a shovel.

"There is something wonderful about digging up your own past."

VERA RUBIN

TWENTIETH CENTURY | BORN 1928 | UNITED STATES
Astronomer

Vera was star-struck. As a girl, she didn't want to sleep. She wanted to stay up and watch the stars from her bedroom window. Her father even helped her construct a telescope out of cardboard. "I faked my way through school," Vera joked. "I turned every assignment into an excuse to write about the cosmos. There was just nothing more interesting to me!"

Vera became an astronomer and changed the way we see the universe. Using a new instrument called a spectrograph, she documented the way that galaxies move. Her findings pointed to the presence of a massive invisible force affecting their rotation speed, providing the first evidence for the existence of dark matter, the stuff that makes up most of our universe.

Vera was a religious Jew whose faith shaped her approach to science. "I'm Jewish," she said. "I believe that science should be looked upon as something that helps us understand our role in the universe."

But Vera almost didn't get her chance to study the stars. Few women studied science as seriously as Vera wanted to. So, she faced many obstacles in pursuing her passion.

Vera was discouraged by teachers, rejected by graduate programs, and denied basic necessities like bathrooms. There weren't even women's restrooms in the astronomy observatories where she worked long hours performing research. But Vera wasn't deterred. She cut out a paper skirt and taped it to the figure of the man on the bathroom door sign, making it a women's room!

Remembering the obstacles she faced, Vera took it upon herself to champion **equal rights** for women in science. She mentored emerging astronomers and involved them in her work. "It is well known," she said, "that I am available twenty-four hours a day to women astronomers." Vera not only unraveled cosmic mysteries. She made it possible for other women to do the same.

"It's possible to be brilliant and also helpful to others as we make our way."

YALTA

TALMUDIC ERA | AROUND 250 | BABYLONIA

Talmudic Sage

In ancient Babylonia, women were expected to keep quiet. But Yalta, a strong and spirited woman, broke the silence, broke the rules, and broke a great many other things.

The Talmud recorded important conversations between rabbis of the time about Jewish law. Few women are mentioned in the Talmud, but Yalta appears several times, refusing to be ignored. In the text, Yalta challenges rabbis and persuades them with her wisdom. She even steps in to protect the honor of her husband.

The Talmud tells the story of a man named Ulla, who visited the home of Yalta and her husband, Rabbi Nahman. At the end of the meal, a special blessing cup was passed around the table. When drinking from the blessing cup, the guests would pray for what they wanted, like health and long life.

When Rabbi Nahman asked the visitor Ulla to pass the cup to his wife, Yalta, he refused. "There is no need," said Ulla. Women don't bless themselves; they only become blessed when their husbands bless them, he argued. Ulla felt it was wasteful for Yalta to drink from the cup.

Furious, Yalta ran to her wine storehouse and smashed four hundred barrels of wine. She wanted to show her guest that it was the mitzvah and not the wine that was important to her. What she desired was to fulfill the commandment of blessing and honoring God.

After Yalta's dramatic actions, her husband again turned to the visitor. "Please send her another cup," he requested. In mockery, Ulla found a less beautiful cup and passed it to Yalta. "This is a cup of blessing," he offered. But Yalta would have none of Ulla's insincerity. "From travelers come tall tales and from rag pickers lice," she replied in disdain, scolding him for his insulting actions.

The numeric value of her Hebrew name is the same as the Hebrew word **emet**, meaning truth. According to commentary, her dramatic actions were truthful and right. With strong words and ways, Yalta fought for generations of women's blessings to be heard and ensured that the name Yalta would never be forgotten.

"From travelers come tall tales and from rag pickers lice." – Berakhot 51b

ZIVIA LUBETKIN & RONI ZUCKERMAN

TWENTIETH CENTURY | BORN 1914   TWENTIETH CENTURY | BORN 1981
            BELARUS   ISRAEL

Jewish Defenders

Every week, they met in a different secret location. As the clouds darkened over the Jews of Europe in the years leading up to World War II, Jewish teens of the Labor Zionist movements huddled in basements, storerooms, and empty warehouses to dream of a brighter future in a national home in the Land of Israel. As history had shown them, no one would save the Jews but the Jews. If they wanted a state, they would need to create it with their own hands.

When World War II broke out, these Zionist dreamers led Jewish resistance efforts against the Nazis. As a young woman, Zivia was a Labor Zionist leader and oversaw the training of new recruits. When the Nazis imprisoned nearly half a million Jews in the Warsaw Ghetto, she bravely left a safer area of Poland to enter the ghetto and join those fighting the Nazis. Zivia was responsible for communicating with groups on the outside, negotiating for funds, and coordinating evacuations.

As the situation worsened, the resistance shifted to an active defense. Zivia helped command the **Warsaw Ghetto Uprising**, a daring act of resistance by seven hundred young Jewish fighters. It was the largest uprising by Jews during World War II and the first major revolt against German occupation in Europe.

For nearly a month, they bravely fought the mightiest army in Europe with little more than pistols, a few rifles, and homemade grenades. Victory was impossible, but Zivia and the other leaders of the revolt were determined to fight back. As the ghetto went up in flames, Zivia helped survivors escape through the underground sewers.

At the end of the war, Zivia moved to the *Yishuv* and established Kibbutz Lohamei HaGeta'ot, the Ghetto Fighters' kibbutz. There, thirty-five years later, Zivia's granddaughter Roni was born. Roni grew up to become the first female fighter pilot in the Israeli Air Force. She was determined, like her grandmother, to do all she could to defend the Jewish people.

"We resisted."
– Zivia Lubetkin

Frida Alexandr
AMERICAS

Frida Alexandr was an Ashkenazi writer of Russian descent raised in a Brazilian colony.

CHUTZPAH

From the bustling streets of Buenos Aires

Chutzpah Girls hail from

Bruria Elnecavé
ARGENTINA

Annalouise Paul
AUSTRALIA

Maria Altmann
AUSTRIA

Yalta
BABYLONIA

Houda Nonoo
BAHRAIN

Zivia Lubetkin
BELARUS

Frida Alexandr
BRAZIL

Judy Feld Carr
CANADA

Claudia Roden
EGYPT

Ashager Araro
ETHIOPIA

Alice Shalvi
GERMANY

Asenath Barzani
KURDISTAN

Edith Eger
HUNGARY

Flora Sassoon
INDIA

Annie Cohen Kopchovks
LATVIA

Ada Yonath
ISRAEL

Benvenida Abravenel
ITALY

Rebecca
MESOPOTAMIA

Chani Lifshitz
NEPAL

Ashager Araro
AFRICA

Ashager Araro is an Ethiopian Israeli activist from the Beta Israel community.

Where is *your* family from?

Laura Margolis Jarblum
OTTOMAN EMPIRE

GIRLS
ARE WORLDWIDE!

...to the rugged mountains of Yemen,
...every corner of the globe.

Bracha Kapach
ASIA

Bracha Kapach was a Yemenite Mizrahi activist who immigrated to pre-State Israel.

⭐ Leah Goldberg	⭐ Ida Nudel
PRUSSIA	RUSSIA

⭐ Helen Suzman	⭐ Ruth Dreifuss	⭐ Gisele Braka
SOUTH AFRICA	SWITZERLAND	TUNISIA

⭐ Golda Meir	⭐ Angela Buxton	⭐ Anne Neuberger
UKRAINE	UNITED KINGDOM	UNITED STATES

⭐ Chana Leviev	⭐ Bracha Kapach
UZBEKISTAN	YEMEN

⭐ Esther
PERSIA

⭐ Malka Braverman
POLAND

⭐ Doña Gracia Nasi
PORTUGAL

Doña Gracia Nasi
EUROPE

Doña Gracia Nasi was a Portuguese Sephardic businesswoman and philanthropist.

Annalouise Paul
OCEANIA

Annalouise Paul is an Australian dancer-choreographer with Ashkenazi and Sephardi roots.

WRITE YOUR
CHUTZPAH STORY

HELLO, GORGEOUS!
DRAW YOUR PORTRAIT

GLOSSARY

Achrayut: Our personal responsibility and moral duty to help others in need.

Aliyah: Stepping up to read Torah in synagogue or to move to Israel and make it home.

Antisemitism: Hostility or hatred of Jews, ranging from a cruel joke to an act of violence.

Ashkenazi: Jews from Eastern Europe. *Famous for bubbies who love you with kugel.*

Balfour Declaration: Britain's promise to create a national home for Jews.

Bat Mitzvah: Ceremony for girls taking on Jewish adult responsibilities. *Mazal tov!*

Beit HaMikdash: Holy Temple in Jerusalem, Judaism's most sacred place.

Beit Midrash: House of study for serious learning and debates on Jewish texts.

Bene Israel: A Jewish community in India; legend says it was started by shipwrecked traders.

Beta Israel: Ethiopian Jewish community established before the Talmud was compiled.

Berakhah: Blessing or prayer for God's help or giving thanks, like *HaMotzi* before a meal.

Bukharan: Central Asian Jewish community from today's Uzbekistan and Tajikistan.

Challah: Traditional braided bread for Shabbat and holidays. *Makes great French toast.*

Chesed: Mitzvah of doing selfless acts of kindness to help others.

Chutzpah: The daring to live or act boldly.

Coexistence: Different groups living side by side in peace and harmony.

Concentration Camp: Place where Jews were imprisoned and killed in the Holocaust.

Converso: Jew forced to convert to Christianity during the Spanish Inquisition.

Convert: Non-Jew who chooses Judaism and adopts the Jewish faith and way of life.

Daf Yomi: Daily study of a page of Talmud, connecting Jews worldwide.

Dati: Hebrew for an observant Jew strictly following Jewish laws and customs.

Diaspora: Scattering of Jews from the Land of Israel to places all around the world.

Emancipation: Granting rights and freedom to an oppressed person or group.

Emet: Hebrew for truth. Speak honestly and act authentically.

Equal Rights: When everyone has the same rights and chances, regardless of identity.

Feminism: Belief in gender equality, the same rights and chances for men and women.

Firzogerin: Yiddish for a knowledgeable and capable female prayer leader.

Ghetto: Neighborhood where Jews were forced to live often in cramped conditions.

God: Singular, all-powerful, eternal force that created the universe and can't be defined.

Haganah: Jewish defense group of the *Yishuv* before the creation of the State of Israel.

Haketia: Language of Sephardic Jews mixing Spanish, Hebrew, Arabic, and French.

Halakhah: Jewish religious laws and traditions that guide our daily life and behavior.

Hanukkah: Festival of light celebrating the rededication of the Beit HaMikdash.

Haredi: Ultra-Orthodox Jews who strictly follow religious laws and traditions.

Hasidism: Joyful, mystical branch of *haredi* Judaism devoted to a rebbe, or spiritual leader.

HaTikvah: National anthem of the State of Israel about the long-standing hope of return.

Hava Nagilah: Lively Hebrew folk dance and song played at many Jewish *simchas*.

Hebrew: Ancient biblical language now spoken by Jews in the State of Israel.

Holocaust: Tragic murder of six million Jews in Europe during World War II. *Never again.*

Ima: Hebrew for mother. *The one who fills the heart, soul, and belly of her family.*

Immigrant: Brave person who moves to live in a new and foreign country.

Israel Defense Forces (IDF): The military that secures and defends the State of Israel.

Ladino: Language spoken by Sephardic Jews, blending mostly Spanish and Hebrew.

Land of Israel: Historic homeland to which Jews longed to return for millenia.

Lay Leader: Volunteer who guides and supports an organization.

Jewish: Belonging to the Jewish people whether by birth or conversion.

Judea: Ancestral land of the Jewish people, originally home to the tribe of Judah.

Kibbutz: Community in Israel where members share work and life.

Kosher: Foods allowed according to Jewish law, like no bacon or cheeseburgers.

Midrash: Stories and interpretations explaining gaps in Jewish texts.

Mitzvah: Religious commandment, like honoring your parents or visiting the sick.

Mizrahi: Jews from the Middle East and North Africa, known for *hamin* stew on Shabbat.

Morah: Respectful term for a female teacher, often used when teaching religious texts.

Mossad: Israel's super-secret spy agency, like the James Bond movies but in real life.

Nazis: Antisemitic followers of Adolf Hitler, who perpetrated the Holocaust.

Neshamah: Your soul, the divine spark that lights up your body and makes you unique.

Nevi'im: Hebrew for prophets. Section of the Jewish Bible with their stories and lessons.

Oral Law: Laws taught to Moses by God at Mount Sinai alongside the written Torah.

Ordain: To officially confer the honored title of rabbi.

Persian: People from Persia, today's Iran, where an ancient Jewish community thrived.

Passover: Holiday commemorating the Israelites' liberation from slavery in Egypt.

Persecution: When a group is treated badly, often because of their religion or ethnicity.

Philanthropy: Generously giving money, time, or resources to help others.

Posek: Rabbinic expert who determines religious rules and answers questions on Jewish law.

Prophetess: Woman who delivers messages and predictions directly from God.

Purim: Festive holiday commemorating Esther's bravery that saved the Jewish people.

Quota: Limit on how many can join a group, like the number of Jews allowed in a club.

Rabbi: Respected and knowledgeable Jewish scholar, teacher, or spiritual leader.

Rashi: French scholar who wrote commentaries on the Tanakh and Talmud.

Refugee: Person forced to flee their home in search of safety from persecution or war.

Refusenik: Jew denied permission to leave the Soviet Union and come to Israel.

Resistance: Underground movement to fight an oppressive force or government.

Restitution: Apologizing or paying for harm done, like art stolen in the Holocaust.

Rosh HaShanah: Jewish New Year and time of personal reflection. *Shanah tovah!*

Savta: Hebrew for grandmother, often known to cover your face with lipstick kisses.

Shabbat: Weekly day of rest beginning Friday night – *turn your phone off and soul on.*

Shtetl: Small Jewish village in Eastern Europe, like Anatevka in *Fiddler on the Roof.*

Sephardi: Jews of Spanish and Portuguese origin, who spoke languages like Ladino.

Shelichah: Hebrew for a female emissary who represents a Jewish cause worldwide.

Six-Day War: Conflict between Israel and neighboring countries in 1967.

Spanish Inquisition: 1492 persecution and expulsion of Jews from the Spanish Kingdom.

State of Israel: Modern country of the Jewish people in their ancestral homeland.

Stereotype: A widely held, simplified, and often unfair belief about a group of people.

Synagogue: Where Jews pray, gather, and shmooze; sometimes called temple or shul.

Talmud: Jewish laws and commentary combining the Mishnah and Gemara.

Tanakh: Hebrew Bible containing the three sections of Torah, Prophets, and Writings.

Tefillah: Connecting with God through prayer, whether in synagogue or in your heart.

Ten Commandments: God's top ten rules, the ultimate go-to moral handbook.

Tenement: Crowded, run-down apartment, often housing new immigrants in a big city.

Tikkun Olam: Doing good deeds to repair our broken world and make it whole again.

Tolerance: Accepting the differences of others without prejudice or judgment.

Torah: Book containing the teachings and laws of God, given to Moses on Mount Sinai.

Tzedek: Hebrew for justice; making things fair and right for everyone.

Warsaw Ghetto Uprising: Brave Jewish resistance against the Nazis during World War II.

World War II: Devastating war involving many countries, when the Holocaust happened.

Yeshivah: School where young Jewish adults study Torah and other Jewish subjects.

Yiddish: Language spoken by Ashkenazi Jews combining Hebrew, German, and humor.

Yishuv: Jewish community in the Land of Israel before the State of Israel's founding.

Yom HaAtzma'ut: Israeli Independence Day, often celebrated with a barbecue!

Zionist: Proud advocate for the existence of a Jewish state in the Land of Israel.

ILLUSTRATORS

Bella Leyn is an Israeli illustrator, originally from Moscow. She graduated from the Moscow State University of Printing Arts and the British Higher School of Art and Design. She volunteers as an art director for Dayenu Media. Bella created the portraits of Angela Buxton, Bruria Benbassat de Elnecavé, Emma Lazarus, Houda Nonoo, Moran Samuel, Roya Hakakian, Ruth Dreifuss, and Sheyna Gifford.

Dafna Barzilay is a Tel Aviv-based product designer by day and illustrator by night. She uses a variety of techniques, from digital collage to handmade paper cutouts. Dafna created the portraits of Ada Yonath, Annie Cohen Kopchovsky, Barbra Streisand, Beatie Deutsch, Deborah Lipstadt, Flora Sassoon, Henrietta Szold, Judy Feld Carr, Linoy Ashram, Ofek Rishon, Rivka Ravitz, Ruth Bader Ginsburg, and Shoshana Cardin.

Diana Leonie was born in London and is now a Jerusalem-based artist. She developed an original technique of hand-dyed papers and creates collage and mixed-medium works of Jewish texts and themes. Diana created the portraits of Adina Bar-Shalom, Benvenida Abravanel, Edith Eger, Grace Aguilar, Hannah Rachel Verbermacher, Leah Goldberg, the Rothschild Women, Sarah Schenirer, and Temerl Bergson.

Liat Popovich is an Israeli illustrator and graduate of the Bezalel Academy of Arts and Design. Her creations use bold colors and playful twists. Liat created the portraits of Alice Shalvi, Batya Sperling Milner, Chani Lifshitz, Frida Alexandr, Gal Gadot, Golda Meir, Inbal Lieberman, Judith Leiber, Laura Margolis Jarblum, Michelle Farber, Rachel Freier, Rose Schneiderman, Ruth Handler with Ellie Goldstein, the Spiritual Leaders, and the authors.

Jacqueline Nicholls is a London-based visual artist and Jewish educator. She uses her art to engage with traditional Jewish ideas in nontraditional ways. She has a master's in fine art from Central Saint Martins. Jacqueline created the portraits of Annalouise Paul, Chana Leviev, Ida Nudel, Judith Montefiore, Lala Tamar, Lori Palatnik, Maria Altmann, the Polgar Sisters, Rosalie Silberman Abella, and Rosalyn Yalow.

Julia Scherer is a Brazilian illustrator and animator living in Jerusalem. Her works range from short films and comics to posters and book illustrations. Julia loved working on

Anne Ross, whose boldness inspired the silk screen–like, layered artwork with strong contrasting colors. Julia created the portraits of Anne Ross and Emmy Noether.

Moran Yogev is an Ethiopian-Israeli illustrator and graduate of the Minshar School of Art in Tel Aviv. She illustrates books and magazines and specializes in print techniques such as linocuts and foam stamps. She lives in Kibbutz Hagoshrim in northern Israel with her husband and children. Moran created the portraits of Kira Radinsky, Noa Tishby, Shulamit Levenberg, Sivan Rahav-Meir, and Vera Rubin.

Rebecca Adler is a fine artist based outside of Philadelphia. Her paintings celebrate women's strength, vulnerability, and grace with bold shapes and saturated hues. She enjoyed painting Queen Esther and delving into the colors of royal garments, which play an important role in the story. Rebecca created the portraits of Anne Frank, Bella Abzug, Claudia Roden, Esther, Gisele Braka, Miriam Schapira-Luria, and Nechama Leibowitz.

Rinat Gilboa is a Jerusalem-based illustrator, graphic designer, and lecturer. Her creative fields connect the worlds of design, illustration, and art – from postage stamps and exhibition design to maps and curation. She graduated from the Bezalel Academy of Arts and Design with a focus on visual communication and industrial design. Rinat created the portraits of Deborah and Yael, Huldah, Leah, Rachel, Rebecca, Sarah, and Yalta.

Rinat Hadar is an Israeli illustrator, lecturer, and graphic designer with her own design studio. She is a mother of four and has a master of arts from Bezalel Academy of Arts and Design. Rinat created the portraits of Abigail, Bruria, the Daughters of Zelophehad, Glückel of Hameln, Hannah, Judith, Meera Jacob Mahadevan, Miriam, the Printers, Ruth and Naomi, and Shlomtzion, as well as the book cover.

Shiri Algor is a Tel-Aviv-based illustrator and paper designer and a graduate of the Bezalel Academy of Arts and Design. She creates innovative and playful paper designs and spends her days buried under paper, cutting, folding, and assembling her creations by hand. Shiri created the portraits of Ashager Araro, Helen Suzman, Mayim Bialik, Rachel Edri, Margret Rey, and Zivia Lubetkin with Roni Zuckerman.

Tilla Crowne is a London-based artist who uses unorthodox materials like broken eggshells and bioluminescent mushrooms. As a member of a Sephardi community descended from families Doña Gracia saved, Tilla felt a strong connection to her story. Tilla created the portraits of Anne Neuberger, Asenath Barzani, Bracha Kapach, Doña Gracia Nasi, Eliza Davis, Malka Braverman, Rudolphina Menzel, and Trude Dothan.

AUTHORS

Julie Silverstein is a messaging strategist and former speechwriter for the Ambassador of Israel to the United Nations. She received her BA in political science and Hebrew from the University of California, Los Angeles, graduating *summa cum laude*, and attended Harvard University's Kennedy School of Government as a Presidential Scholar. Julie was a US State Department Fulbright Fellow in Israel, Bertelsmann Foundation Fellow, and Wexner Heritage Fellow, and attended classes at the Yakar Beit Midrash and Pardes Institute. Julie grew up in San Francisco and now lives in Jerusalem with her husband and five children. She loves swimming at sunrise and celebrating Shabbat with family and friends.

Julie wrote *Chutzpah Girls* to honor the daring Jewish men and women in her life, like her grandmother, who, as a girl in Germany, bravely confronted the Nazi police to demand the release of her father from unjust detention. She hopes this book will be a key that unlocks the stories of chutzpah in your family. Her favorite Chutzpah Girl is the Yiddish diarist Glückel of Hameln, who carved out the time to write with fourteen children at home.

Tami Schlossberg Pruwer is a brand strategist who loves crafting stories for causes she cares about. At Saatchi & Saatchi she led award-winning brand campaigns for global corporations and the third sector, including Google and the WHO. She holds a BA in political science and French literature from Bar-Ilan University, and an MA in government from Reichman University. Tami is a graduate of Michlalah College and has spent years learning at Matan and Beit Morasha. She is fluent in six languages and has led multiple initiatives to advance upward mobility for women.

Tami was born in Milan, Italy, and grew up in Antwerp, Belgium. She now lives in Tel Aviv with her husband and their two children. Tami can often be found discovering the best coffee, new galleries or attending flamenco classes. Tami comes from and married into lineages of strong Jewish women. She wrote this book in their honor and to inspire her children with the heroines of their heritage. Her favorite Chutzpah Girl is Flora Sassoon. Any Jewish businesswoman traveling the world with her own minyan and shochet is definitely a kindred spirit!

THANK YOU

Chutzpah is more powerful when achieved together. With it, you can scale mountains, but with the *chutzpah* of many, you can move mountains. This book was made possible by the *chutzpah* of many women and men, to whom we are deeply grateful.

We were fortunate to work with the best in Jewish publishing – Matthew Miller and Koren Publishers, and our exceptional team at Koren's Toby Press, Caryn Meltz, Aryeh Grossman, Ashirah Firszt, Tani Bayer, Alex Drucker, Talya Lourie, Esther Shafier, and Debbie Ismail-off, whose unwavering dedication and commitment to excellence made **Chutzpah Girls** possible. We'd also like to acknowledge Lisa Eisen, Rebecca Shafron, and the Schusterman Foundation for their guidance and generous support.

Thank you to our talented illustrators and graphic artists, Abbey Schuyler, Bella Leyn, Dafna Barzilay, Diana Leonie, Jacqueline Nicholls, Julia Scherer, Liat Popovich, Moran Yogev, Nicole Butterfield, Rebecca Adler, Rinat Gilboa, Rinat Hadar, Shiri Algor, and Tilla Crowne, who created with their hands and hearts.

We'd like to express appreciation to our exceptional reviewers, Rabbanit Dr. Sarit Kattan Gribetz, Rabbanit Dr. Ayelet Hoffmann Libson, Rabbanit Sharona Margolin Halickman, Dr. Henry Abramson and Aviva Arad, and our many kid reviewers who could always be counted on for their honest feedback.

We'd also like to thank the many individuals who advised us along the way, including Abbie Greenberg, Adina Mirchin, Anaelle Nowotny, Andrea Wolf, Ben Pery, Rabbi Benji Levy, Dr. Carole Balin, Chaim Motzen, Corinne Shmuel, Ellen Frankel, Eylon Levy, Dr. Gil Troy, Gideon Shaw, Harlene Appelbaum z"l, Hillel Neuer, Ittay Flescher, Dr. James Loeffler, Rabbi Jay Moses, Jeff Rum, Joseph Gitler, Juliet Spitzer, Rabbi Leon Morris, Mandy Kaiser-Blueth, Mark Dubowitz, Dr. Mayim Bialik, Dr. Michal Paz Shimony, Noam Ohana, Oren Charnoff, Rae Ringel, Richard Shapiro, Sarah Hurwitz, Shari Last, Suzanne Patt Benvenisti, Trude Vincent, Dr. Ulrike Offenberg, and Yoav Davis, as well as our legal team at Meitar, David Mirchin and Rebecca Fischer.

We'd like to express utmost gratitude to God for bringing us to this moment and to our friends and family, today and generations past, who inspired us with their chutzpah. Tami would first like to thank her grandparents and great-grandparents, whose brave life stories inspired her interest in chutzpah. Special thanks to her mother, Alisa Majer, and mother-in-law Betty Pruwer who live with unparalleled strength, as well as her sister Eliane, and sister-in-law Fella, for their constant support and insight, and to Anthony as well as her brothers and brother-in-law, for their excitement throughout this journey. To her nieces, Noa, Sara, Naomi, and Miriam, whose middot and humor are unparalleled, this work is crafted with you in mind. Special shout-out to her aunts, uncles, and cousins all around the world, whose chutzpah and authenticity inspired this book.

To the women whose kindness, integrity, wisdom, and chutzpah never cease to inspire, Tami feels deeply privileged to have you in her life: Althea Mirvis, Avital Sterngold, Batsheva Neuer, Becky Strapp, Chana Kraus, Daniella Zeloof, Danielle Holtz, Elisheva Kupferman, Ellie Mochkin, Fleur Barth, Hannah Waxman, Karen Landau, Kreindy Schlaff, Laetitia Zohar, Laura Levi, Leora Jesselson, Paula Kweskin, Rebecca Abeles, Sarah Keyes, Sarah Sofer, Shira Fass, Tali Bollag, Tali Stemmer, Tammy Levy, Tamar Koschitzky, and Tanya Waxman.

She wrote this book for her children, Amalia and Judah, whose playfulness, zest, and love are a constant source of inspiration. May these stories anchor and inspire you as you navigate life. To David, for always supporting her dreams. You are the partner that every Chutzpah Girl deserves. She feels blessed to be so lucky.

Julie would like to give special thanks to her parents, Rabbi Cantor Dr. Linda and Peter Bernstein z"l, and Dr. Gary Stein, her mother and father-in-law Wylie and Dr. Bill Silverstein, her brother Danny, and the wonderful Aronson, Bernstein, Brous, Jagoda, Lavi, Laufer, Newfield, Silverstein, Sinton, Stein, Steinway, Posin, Uhrman, and Youngerwood clans, whose strength and love are without parallel. She is also deeply grateful to friends and supporters from all stages of her life who cheered her along from near and far.

Julie dedicates this book to her dear children, Matan, Noa, Ivria, Lev, and Miri, whose curiosity, love of reading, and Jewish pride inspired her to write it. May you dare to imagine and achieve impossible dreams, and may you always be a light unto the world. And to her husband, Rusty, who encouraged her with his love, brilliance, and wisdom at every step. She feels blessed beyond words.

Finally, we join in thanking our one hundred Chutzpah Girls and their families for trusting us with their stories and all the Chutzpah Kids out there for reading these stories of daring Jewish women. May they inspire you to embrace your heritage with courage, resilience, and boundless determination as you write your own story.

WHAT'S NEXT

Did we leave out your favorite Chutzpah Girl?

One hundred women is nowhere near a complete list of all the Chutzpah Girls who dared to accomplish great things as proud Jewish women. In every era of history, every corner of the world, and every field, Jewish women have had the drive to survive and thrive. We wanted to include them all!

But don't worry. We plan to tell more Chutzpah Girl stories and would love to know who you're interested in learning about.

Do you love singing in the shower? If so, you'll love Edis de Philippe, the mesmerizing soprano who brought opera to the newly established State of Israel.

Are you always in the middle of a craft project? If so, you'll love Dulcea of Worms, the medieval businesswoman who meticulously sewed forty Torah scrolls by hand.

Are you always dreaming of the next great adventure? If so, you'll love Adel Bat Baal Shem Tov, the Early Modern Era mystic who survived a stormy shipwreck.

Or perhaps you'd like to dive deeper into someone you know – a favorite figure from the Torah, a changemaker in your local community, or a leading lady in your own family. It's even possible our next Chutzpah Girl is you! Write to us, support the movement, and join our community at:

Facebook: facebook/chutzpahgirls

Instagram: instagram/wearechutzpahgirls

Website: www.chutzpahgirls.com

Email: info@chutzpahgirls.com

Invite us to speak! We've got chutzpah.